Django 6 Cookbook

Second Edition

Build modern full-stack apps with Django 6, Python 3.12, APIs, authentication, testing, search, and deployment

Clara Stein

Published by: GitforGits

www.gitforgits.com

Printed in India

First Printing: March 2026

ISBN: 978-93-49174-08-5

Cover Design by: Kitten Publishing

Disclaimer:

This book, including all its text, diagrams, and illustrations, is an original work developed for educational and informational purposes. The content is not affiliated with, endorsed by, or sponsored by or any other company, brand, or entity referenced within. All brand names, product names, and trademarks mentioned are the property of their respective owners and are used in a descriptive, educational context only. Every effort has been made to ensure that no copyrighted or trademarked material has been copied or misused in this book. All diagrams and illustrations that are not original have been used with proper attribution and credit to their respective sources.

If you believe that any content in this book infringes upon our copyright or trademark, please contact us immediately at support@gitforgits.com. Upon notification, corrective action will be taken promptly.

Prologue

Some books ask you to read. This one asks you to build.

This distinction matters more than it may first appear. A cookbook is not a narrative you follow from one page to the next waiting for resolution. It is a workbench. You arrive at it with a problem, a curiosity, or a gap in your understanding, and you leave with something that works. The recipes collected here are practical answers to the kind of problems that real Django applications encounter, sometimes on the first day of a project and sometimes deep into the life of a codebase that has grown well beyond its original design.

From its earliest versions, the framework carried a quiet but firm opinion about software. It says that clarity is more valuable than cleverness, that structure prevents more problems than flexibility alone can solve, and that the discipline of fitting your work to a coherent system pays back the effort many times over. These convictions have not softened as Django has matured. If anything, each major release has deepened them. The Django 6 continues that tradition while bringing meaningful new capability to the parts of the framework where real applications most often feel the strain. This book was written to meet that version of Django honestly. The template partials give the presentation layer real composability without the overhead of a full component framework. The built-in task support provides a neater path for background work that previously needed to be carefully put together by third parties. A lot of Django projects don't pay enough attention to browser security when they're dealing with Content Security Policy. It's ASGI-aware deployment and Channels-ready architecture that makes real-time features a natural part of the stack, rather than an exotic addition bolted on from the outside. It's got full-text search and storage-aware file handling, which give you the answers you need to deal with problems that growing applications often face. We chose each of these additions to include them because they reduce friction where it slows down developers.

Still, features are only part of the story. The deeper value of this cookbook lies in the thinking that holds the recipes together. This book is a discipline of knowing where concerns belong, how the layers of an application relate to one another, and how to make decisions today that will still feel sound when requirements shift six months from now. A recipe that teaches you to build a form is also teaching you something about validation, trust, and user intent. A recipe about deployment is also a recipe about assumptions, infrastructure contracts, and the gap between development behavior and production reality. This book tries to honor that depth. It does not present topics as islands. It presents them as parts of a connected system, because that is what a web application actually is. The recipes are organized to reflect the natural arc of application development. Each chapter builds on what came before, but the book is also designed to serve readers who arrive looking for a specific answer rather than reading straight through. If you need to understand how to handle file uploads safely, that recipe stands on its own. If you need to add full-text search to an existing application, you can go there directly. The structure respects both ways of reading because both are legitimate.

To me, there are two kinds of readers who are likely to find this book useful, and they will use it differently.

First are those who are early in their Django experience, approaching the framework with working knowledge but not yet a strong intuition for how the pieces fit together at scale. And, then therei si another set of readers who come to this book with significant prior Django experience, perhaps from an earlier version of the framework or from a codebase that has carried its original patterns longer than it probably should. What both readers share, is the need for a book that takes production seriously from the start. This is not a book that reserves deployment, security, and testing for final chapters as though they were decorative concerns applied after the real work is done.

One more thing deserves to be said before the recipes begin. No cookbook can replace the judgment that comes from building real software under real constraints. What it can do is sharpen that judgment. It can reduce the time you spend solving problems that have already been solved well. It can give you a richer vocabulary of patterns so that when you face something new, you have more tools for recognizing its shape and choosing a sound approach. It can help you ask better questions earlier in a project, which is where the cost of a wrong direction is still recoverable.

The workbench is ready. The problems are real. The framework is capable.

Let us begin.

Content

Preface

This practical second edition will help you solve the real challenges of full stack development with focused, hands-on recipes. If you're shaping data models, building forms and templates, designing APIs with Django REST Framework, securing authentication flows, or preparing your project for production, this book will show you precisely and systematically to overcome common obstacles and achieve successful results.

This edition is fully updated for Django 6 and Python 3.12, allowing you to leverage the framework's cutting-edge capabilities in real projects. You will learn to use Django 6 features such as template partials, the Tasks framework for email-driven workflows, built-in Content Security Policy support, improved form and widget patterns, ASGI-aware deployment, and stronger PostgreSQL integration for search and performance. As you progress, you will undoubtedly develop superior testing, security, storage, API, real-time features and deployment approaches.

This cookbook is for developers who want practical progress, with reusable solutions for building secure, maintainable, and production-ready Django applications that can support today's web and full stack development needs.

In this book you will learn to:

- Build modern Django 6 web applications with Python 3.12 confidently.
- Design robust models, relationships, constraints, and PostgreSQL-backed data layers.
- Create maintainable views, templates, partials, and dynamic user experiences.
- Develop reusable, validated, and secure forms for real application workflows.
- Implement authentication, authorization, sessions, and advanced account management flows.
- Build REST APIs with Django REST Framework.
- Add real-time features with Channels, ASGI, and WebSocket-based communication.
- Apply testing, CI, debugging, and deployment skill for production readiness.
- Secure applications with HTTPS, CSP, safe cookies, and defensive defaults.
- Optimize performance with caching, indexing, full-text search, and efficient queries.

GitforGits

Prerequisites

This book is designed for python developer, backend developers and full stack developers who want reusable solutions for building secure, maintainable, and production-ready Django apps that can support today's web and full stack development needs.

Codes Usage

Are you in need of some helpful code examples to assist you in your programming and documentation? Look no further! Our book offers a wealth of supplemental material, including code examples and exercises.

Not only is this book here to aid you in getting the job done, but you have our permission to use the example code in our programs and documentation. However, please note that if you are reproducing a significant portion of the code, we do require you to contact us for permission.

But don't worry, using several chunks of code from this book in our program or answering a question by citing our book and quoting example code does not require permission. But if you do choose to give credit, an attribution typically includes the title, author, publisher, and ISBN. For example, "Django 6 Cookbook, Second Edition by Clara Stein".

If you are unsure whether our intended use of the code examples falls under fair use or the permissions outlined above, please do not hesitate to reach out to us at support@gitforgits.com.

We are happy to assist and clarify any concerns.

Acknowledgement

I owe a tremendous debt of gratitude to GitforGits, for their unflagging enthusiasm and wise counsel throughout the entire process of writing this book. Their knowledge and careful editing helped make sure the piece was useful for people of all reading levels and comprehension skills. In addition, I'd like to thank everyone involved in the publishing process for their efforts in making this book a reality. Their efforts, from copyediting to advertising, made the project what it is today.

Finally, I'd like to express my gratitude to everyone who has shown me unconditional love and encouragement throughout my life. Their support was crucial to the completion of this book. I appreciate our help with this endeavour and our continued interest in my career.

CHAPTER 1: GETTING STARTED WITH DJANGO 6

Overview

This chapter opens the door to Django in a way that feels immediate, practical, and rewarding from the very first command we run. We will not begin with heavy theory or long explanations about framework internals. Rather, we will begin by creating a clean Python 3.12 environment, installing Django 6.0, and turning that setup into a working project that we can run in the browser almost right away. From there, we will start shaping the early structure of our GitforGits app so that each new piece has a clear purpose and a natural place to live. We will see how Django organizes work through projects and apps, and we will use that structure to keep our code tidy from the beginning instead of trying to fix disorder later.

As we move forward, we will define our first model, use the Django admin to manage it, route requests to views, render data with templates, and then accept user input through forms. Every recipe in this chapter will build directly on the one before it, so the learning path will feel less like separate demonstrations and more like one steady live development teaching altogether. By the end of the chapter, we will not only understand the core building blocks that power a Django application, but we will also have a real starting version of GitforGits running with data, pages, and input handling in place.

Recipe 1: Django 6.0 Installation and Virtual Environment

The first step to begin with Django is the very first creation of a specific workspace for our project. And, this is needed, because an isolated environment prevents package conflicts, reduces accidental version drift, and helps us keep our project reproducible from the very beginning. We are targeting Python 3.12 or later and a Django 6.0.x installation. The Django's official tutorial for version 6.0 is written for Python 3.12 and later, and the 6.0 release notes confirm that Django 6.0 supports Python 3.12, 3.13, and 3.14.

Creating Virtual Environment

Before creating the virtual environment, we should verify the interpreter that will drive our work in the rest of the chapter. That check matters because if a machine still points python to an older release, we could install the right Django version but still end up with confusing compatibility issues later. For Django 6.0, we want Python 3.12 or later, and we want our shell session to show us that clearly before we move ahead. The Django's installation guide still recommends installing an official release with **pip** inside a virtual environment as shown below:

```
python --version
```

If the shell does not return a Python 3.12.x interpreter, we can use the explicit executable:

```
python3.12 --version
```

After this, we can create the isolated workspace for GitforGits. We will continue to name the environment '**gitforgits**', since that keeps the rest of the chapter and the sample project consistent.

After the environment is created, we activate it so every install and Django command in this chapter belongs to this project alone rather than leaking into the system interpreter or another unrelated workspace.

```
python -m venv gitforgits
```

Installing Django 6.0

Once the environment is active, we will install Django 6.0 release explicitly so that our commands, generated files, and screenshots stay aligned throughout the learning. And after installation, we will verify the version immediately.

```
python -m pip install "Django==6.0.*"
python -m django --version
```

With this, we have a dedicated Python 3.12 environment with Django 6.0 installed and ready for the rest of the chapter. This is the only setup baseline we need, and from here onward we can assume that our environment is active and correctly configured instead of repeating installation steps again and again.

Recipe 2: Creating First Django Project

Now that our Python 3.12 virtual environment is active and Django 6.0 is installed, we can begin building **GitforGits** web app. So here, in this recipe, we will create the project skeleton, introduce the files that make a Django project run, and will then give the first visible sign that our framework setup is healthy.

As per the latest release notes, there is a new adjustment in Django 6.0 which is, that it defaults **`DEFAULT_AUTO_FIELD`** to **`BigAutoField`**. This makes the project template a little cleaner than before (I just wanted you to be aware of, in case you are already a Django professional like me).

Structuring Project

To start with, we move into the directory where we want the work to live, and then create the project. Here, we will use using **`python -m django startproject`** as shown below:

```
python -m django startproject gitforgits
```

It will generate the familiar project files that we will keep returning to. Here, **manage.py** remains our command-line utility for project tasks. The inner **gitforgits/** directory remains the home of the project package, including **settings.py**, **urls.py**, **asgi.py**, and **wsgi.py**.

```
├── manage.py
└── gitforgits/
    ├── __init__.py
    ├── settings.py
    ├── urls.py
    ├── asgi.py
    └── wsgi.py
```

Running Development Server

The development server remains the fastest way to confirm that our environment, installed packages, and generated project files all agree with one another. That early feedback matters because it gives us confidence that the foundation is healthy before we begin creating apps, models, views, templates, and forms.

So here, we start the development server and open the local site in the browser. When the Django welcome page appears, it confirms that our Python version, Django installation, and project scaffold are all wired up correctly.

```
python manage.py runserver
```

Now visit:

```
http://127.0.0.1:8000/
```

After this, the project is running and ready to grow. The value of this recipe is not only that it creates files for us. It also establishes the command rhythm we are going to follow while learning Django. We create, run, inspect, and then extend.

Recipe 3: Structure of Django Apps

With the gitforgits project now running, the next important step is to understand how Django organizes its components.

Well, a Django project is not one giant block of code. It is usually a collection of focused apps that work together toward a common goal. That modular architecture is one of Django's most practical strengths because it helps us keep features grouped by responsibility instead of allowing the codebase to turn into a tangled knot. For GitforGits, we will create an app named collaboration, in which we will inspect the structure Django gives us, and then register it in the project.

Creating First App

We continue in the same project directory and use **manage.py** to generate the first app. That command still produces the exact kind of scaffold we want in an opening chapter because it gives us a place for models, views, tests, migrations, and admin integration without forcing us to invent a structure ourselves. So here, we are not merely adding a directory, rather we are introducing one of Django's most important habits, which is to keep related behavior together in a focused application package.

```
python manage.py startapp collaboration
```

The generated structure will look like this:

```
collaboration/
├── __init__.py
├── admin.py
├── apps.py
├── migrations/
│   └── __init__.py
├── models.py
├── tests.py
└── views.py
```

Registering App

Each file in the app serves a practical role. The **models.py** will describe our data. The **views.py** will hold request-handling logic. The **admin.py** will expose selected models to the admin interface. The **tests.py** gives us a home for verification. The **migrations/** tracks schema evolution. And, the **apps.py** contains the application configuration. The Django's applications documentation explains that apps can be referenced in **INSTALLED_APPS** either by application package or by configuration class, and the **apps.py** convention exists to make configuration easier to discover and load.

So here, we open **gitforgits/settings.py** and update **INSTALLED_APPS**:

```
INSTALLED_APPS = [
    "django.contrib.admin",
    "django.contrib.auth",
    "django.contrib.contenttypes",
    "django.contrib.sessions",
    "django.contrib.messages",
    "django.contrib.staticfiles",
    "collaboration.apps.CollaborationConfig",
]
```

This recipe teaches that, each app should encapsulate a cohesive set of features or behaviors. It helps to keep a Django project organized and scalable. It remains one of the cleanest ways to introduce Django's project architecture, and hence our best move is to preserve it and only tighten the registration detail slightly.

Recipe 4: Defining Data for Models

Once our project and first app are in place, the next step is to define the data models. The models define the structure of our database tables and allow Django's ORM to work with the database using Python classes rather than raw SQL for every operation. For GitforGits, a Snippet model still makes perfect sense because code snippets remain the core content object in the application.

Creating and Registering Snippets

The models live inside Django apps, so we begin by creating an app for code snippets if it does not already exist. After creating the app, we should register it immediately rather than leaving that step implicit. This small improvement makes the solution more self-contained and reduces the chance that you reached the migration before Django is actually aware of the app.

```
python manage.py startapp snippets
```

Next, we then add it to **INSTALLED_APPS** in **gitforgits/settings.py**:

```
INSTALLED_APPS = [
    "django.contrib.admin",
    "django.contrib.auth",
```

```
    "django.contrib.contenttypes",
    "django.contrib.sessions",
    "django.contrib.messages",
    "django.contrib.staticfiles",
    "collaboration.apps.CollaborationConfig",
    "snippets.apps.SnippetsConfig",
]
```

Defining Model

Next ,we then open **snippets/models.py** and define the Snippet model. The Django's models documentation still describes a model as the single, definitive source of information about our data. So here, we define the title, code body, language, and creation timestamp as fields on the model, and we keep **__str__()**, so the model reads well in the admin and shell. We do not declare a primary key ourselves because Django handles that for us automatically.

In Django 6.0, the default auto field behavior uses **BigAutoField**, which is now built into the defaults rather than being written explicitly into project and app templates. Such a detail changes the generated configuration slightly, but the model authoring experience remains refreshingly straightforward.

```
from django.db import models
class Snippet(models.Model):
    title = models.CharField(max_length=100)
    code = models.TextField()
    language = models.CharField(max_length=50)
    created_at = models.DateTimeField(auto_now_add=True)
    def __str__(self):
        return self.title
```

Applying Migration

Next, we then create and apply the migration:

```
python manage.py makemigrations snippets
python manage.py migrate
```

And finally, we then register the model in **snippets/admin.py**:

```
from django.contrib import admin
from .models import Snippet
admin.site.register(Snippet)
```

This whole thing now gives us our first real data structure in the project, and that is the point where GitforGits starts to feel like an application. We have a model, a database table, and a record type that later recipes can display, edit, search, submit, and manage.

Recipe 5: Customizing Admin Interface

To manage our site's content, the Django admin still remains one of the most useful built-in parts of the framework. For GitforGits, an admin interface for snippets makes it easier to create, inspect, update, and remove records while we are still building the public-facing side of the application.

Creating Superuser

To begin with, we will first create a superuser, run the development server, and visit the admin site.

```
python manage.py createsuperuser
python manage.py runserver
```

Then open:

```
http://127.0.0.1:8000/admin/
```

Once we log in, we gain an instant back-office interface for our registered models. This moment is still valuable in a beginner chapter because it shows us the real project data through a polished interface before we have built many custom screens of our own.

Customizing Snippet Admin

Our real improvement comes from shaping how the Snippet model appears inside the admin. It has **list_display**, **list_filter**, **search_fields**, a custom form, and fieldsets. The Django 6.0 includes admin refinements such as **AdminSite.password_change_form** attribute and changes to message-level styling. It tells us that admin remains an actively maintained part of Django.

```
from django import forms
from django.contrib import admin, messages
from .models import Snippet
class SnippetAdminForm(forms.ModelForm):
    class Meta:
        model = Snippet
        fields = "__all__"
        help_texts = {
            "code": "Enter our code snippet here.",
        }
@admin.register(Snippet)
class SnippetAdmin(admin.ModelAdmin):
    form = SnippetAdminForm
    list_display = ("title", "language", "created_at")
    list_filter = ("language",)
    search_fields = ("title", "code")
    fieldsets = (
        (
            None,
            {
                "fields": ("title", "language"),
            },
        ),
        (
            "Content",
            {
                "fields": ("code",),
                "description": "Section for the code snippet
itself.",
```

```
            },
        ),
    )
    def save_model(self, request, obj, form, change):
        super().save_model(request, obj, form, change)
        self.message_user(
            request,
            "Snippet saved successfully.",
            level=messages.SUCCESS,
        )
```

This solution still proves one of Django's best practical advantages. It can turn our model into a usable internal interface quickly, and then refine that interface in targeted ways instead of building administration pages from scratch. It truly gives us immediate leverage and makes the project feel useful long before the public application surface is fully developed.

Recipe 6: Simple URL Routing to Views

The URL remains the gateway into a Django application, and routing remains the mechanism that connects incoming requests to the views that will respond to them. The Django 6.0 still uses **URLconfs** and **path()** to map patterns to view callables. In this recipe, we want a clean route that takes users to a page representing a list of snippets. Here, I want you to focus on the request-to-response chain without too many moving parts at once.

Creating View

To start with, we begin by adding a simple view in **snippets/views.py**. The original approach of returning a plain **HttpResponse** with the snippet titles is still appropriate in this solution because it tests the mechanics of the route without jumping into template rendering too early.

```
from django.http import HttpResponse
from .models import Snippet
def snippet_list(request):
    """A view to display a list of code snippets."""
    snippets = Snippet.objects.all()
```

```
    snippets_list = ", ".join([snippet.title for snippet in snippets])
    return HttpResponse(f"List of Snippets: {snippets_list}")
```

In the above, we query all Snippet objects, join their titles, and return the result. It allows us to see that the route is alive, the view is callable, and the model query works. This sort of directness is valuable at this stage because I want you to see the moving parts separately before we start layering on templates and forms in the next recipes.

Mapping URL Pattern

Now we connect a URL path to that view in **`gitforgits/urls.py`**. The Django's URL routing documentation continues to describe this mapping as one of the central parts of request handling, and that is exactly what we are teaching here. The name argument remains worth including because it gives us a stable symbolic name we can use later in redirects, templates, and reverse lookups. That may look like a small detail in this chapter, but it pays off quickly as the codebase needs stable route references rather than repeated hard-coded paths.

```
from django.contrib import admin
from django.urls import path
from snippets.views import snippet_list
urlpatterns = [
    path("admin/", admin.site.urls),
    path("snippets/", snippet_list, name="snippet_list"),
]
```

After this, we then run the server and visit:

```
http://127.0.0.1:8000/snippets/
```

When the route responds, we confirm that the model, view, URL pattern, and server are now talking to one another.

Recipe 7: Rendering Data with Templates

Now that we have a working view and route, the next natural step is to improve the response that users actually see. A plain text list of snippet titles is enough to prove the route works, but it is not how we want to present data in a real application. The Django's templating system remains one of the cleanest ways to separate presentation from Python logic. In Django 6.0, there is native

template partials through **{% partialdef %}** and **{% partial %}**. They are genuinely useful, but they belong more naturally in the later templates chapter than in this rendering recipe.

So here, in this recipe, we will simply foreshadow the stronger composition tools which we are going to introduce in the later chapters.

Creating Template

So, to begin with, inside the snippets app, we will create a **templates/snippets/** directory and add **snippet_list.html**. The template stays simple, like it loop through snippets, print each title and code pair, and show a fallback message if no snippets exist yet.

```
<!DOCTYPE html>
<html lang="en">
<head>
    <meta charset="UTF-8">
    <title>Snippet List</title>
</head>
<body>
    <h1>List of Snippets</h1>
    <ul>
        {% for snippet in snippets %}
            <li>{{ snippet.title }}: {{ snippet.code }}</li>
        {% empty %}
            <li>No snippets found.</li>
        {% endfor %}
    </ul>
</body>
</html>
```

The Django's template documentation still presents this model of variables and tags as the core of template rendering, and that is precisely what I want you to practice here. Here in this recipe, we are not trying to build a polished design system. Rather, I am aiming to teach you the basic contract between the view's context and the template's output.

Rendering Template from View

Next, we will update the **snippet_list** view so it uses the **render()** shortcut rather than returning plain text. It keeps the view focused on gathering data while the template takes care of presentation. This division of labor is one of Django's most approachable design choices, and it is the real lesson of this recipe.

```
from django.shortcuts import render
from .models import Snippet
def snippet_list(request):
    snippets = Snippet.objects.all()
    return render(request, "snippets/snippet_list.html",
{"snippets": snippets})
```

The Django 6.0 supports native partial definitions and direct rendering of template fragments using **template.html#partial_name**. It is useful, especially for reusable UI fragments and partial page updates, but for now, in this chapter, we will keep the rendering example simple and confidence-building.

Next, we then reload the **/snippets/page** in the browser and we should now see a proper HTML page instead of a plain string response. This transition matters because it is the moment where our application begins to feel like a real web interface rather than an internal mechanics test.

Recipe 8: Up and Running with Forms and User Input

To make the GitforGits app interactive, we may need to accept user-submitted snippets rather than only displaying data that was created elsewhere. The Django's forms framework offers one of the most efficient ways to do that. The Django 6.0 does introduce one forms-related change, which is that the default scheme for **forms.URLField** is now https. And, the old **FORMS_URLFIELD_ASSUME_HTTPS** transitional setting is removed. This specific example does not include a **URLField**, so we do not need to rewrite the code because of that change.

Defining Modelform and View

So, we begin with a **ModelForm** class in **snippets/forms.py**:

```
# snippets/forms.py
from django import forms
from .models import Snippet
```

```
class SnippetForm(forms.ModelForm):
    class Meta:
        model = Snippet
        fields = ["title", "code", "language"]
# snippets/views.py
from django.shortcuts import render, redirect
from .forms import SnippetForm
def submit_snippet(request):
    if request.method == "POST":
        form = SnippetForm(request.POST)
        if form.is_valid():
            form.save()
            return redirect("snippet_list")
    else:
        form = SnippetForm()
    return render(request, "snippets/submit_snippet.html",
{"form": form})
```

This pattern remains current and is still one of the cleanest ways to bridge model definitions and user input handling. In the view, we handle both **GET** and **POST** requests. When the request is **GET**, we show the empty form. When the request is **POST**, we bind the submitted data, validate it, save the object if valid, and then redirect to the snippet list.

Creating Template and URL Pattern

Now we create the form template and register its route. The template remains intentionally minimal because this chapter is about getting the full request-validate-save cycle working, and not about advanced rendering customization. The use of **{{ form.as_p }}** is still a fine opening move even though Django's forms API offers more granular rendering approaches now. The route definition also remains simple. We add a **/submit/** path for the form view and keep the existing **/snippets/** path for the list page.

```
<!DOCTYPE html>
<html lang="en">
<head>
```

```
    <meta charset="UTF-8">
    <title>Submit Snippet</title>
</head>
<body>
    <h1>Submit a New Snippet</h1>
    <form method="post">
        {% csrf_token %}
        {{ form.as_p }}
        <button type="submit">Submit</button>
    </form>
</body>
</html>
from django.contrib import admin
from django.urls import path
from snippets.views import snippet_list, submit_snippet
urlpatterns = [
    path("admin/", admin.site.urls),
    path("snippets/", snippet_list, name="snippet_list"),
    path("submit/", submit_snippet, name="submit_snippet"),
]
```

With the development server running, we then visit **`/submit/`**, add a few snippets, and confirm that the records are saved and the browser redirects back to the snippet list page. With this, we have moved from environment setup to a running project, from project to apps, from apps to models, from models to admin, from URLs to templates, and finally from templates to user input.

Summary

In this chapter, we established the foundation of our Django journey by setting up a dedicated Python 3.12 virtual environment and installing Django 6.0 as the framework baseline. We then created the GitforGits project and explored the structure that Django generated for us, which gave us a clear understanding of where settings, URL configuration, and server entry points belonged. After that, we created focused apps to organize our work, registered them properly, and used that structure to define our first meaningful model, Snippet, as the backbone of the application's data.

We then used the Django admin to create an internal management interface, routed browser requests to a view, and replaced a plain text response with template-rendered HTML so that our data could be presented in a cleaner and more useful way. Finally, we connected a ModelForm to the Snippet model so users could submit new records through a safe, validated form workflow. It showed us how Django's major building blocks fit together in practice. Overall, we had moved through environment setup, project creation, app organization, data modeling, administration, routing, rendering, and form handling for a strong and practical base for the more advanced recipes ahead.

CHAPTER 2: IMPLEMENTING MODELS AND DATABASES

Overview

This chapter will take us deeper into Django's model layer and the database patterns that support a growing application. In this, we will move beyond simple model definitions and begin working with the relationship types that shape how real data connects in practice. Through one-to-one, foreign key, many-to-many, and generic relationships, we will learn to represent ownership, classification, extension, and flexible associations in a way that keeps our models expressive and maintainable. We will also explore composite primary keys so we can understand when a row should be identified by more than one field and how that choice will affect querying, migrations, and the way we think about model identity.

Next, we will see custom managers and querysets packaging the common query logic, the signals responding to model events, and soft deletion to preserve records without losing access to them entirely. We will then examine validators, constraints, and transactions so we can protect data integrity with confidence and keep multi-step database operations trustworthy across realistic application workflows every day. After that, we will connect Django to PostgreSQL using psycopg 3 and environment-driven settings, explore connection pools, and will end the chapter with learning how indexes and query optimization helps to stay efficient.

Recipe 1: Handling Complex Model Relationships

To build complex web applications, we often need to model relationships that mirror how real information is connected in practice. In our app or in any other application, a user may have one profile, an author may own many snippets, one snippet may carry many tags, and comments may need to attach themselves to more than one kind of object. The Django gives us a rich set of relationship fields for this exact purpose. And, in this recipe, we will choose the field, shape the way we query, navigate, and extend the data. We will explore the behavior of **`OneToOneField`**, **`ForeignKey`**, **`ManyToManyField`**, and **`GenericForeignKey`**, such that the application appears with a coherent app design.

One-to-One Relationships

A one-to-one relationship is the right choice when one record in a model must correspond to exactly one record in another model. This is especially useful when we want to extend user data without altering the authentication model directly. In our case, a user profile is a natural example because each user can have one profile, and each profile belongs to one user. We will keep the model simple and practical so the intent remains easy to follow. We have remember that we use **`settings.AUTH_USER_MODEL`** rather than importing the user directly. That pattern keeps the model flexible and works well even when a project later switches to a custom user model. We will also add a **`related_name`** so we can move from a user object to the related profile cleanly in our application code.

```
from django.conf import settings
from django.db import models
class UserProfile(models.Model):
    user = models.OneToOneField(
        settings.AUTH_USER_MODEL,
        on_delete=models.CASCADE,
        related_name="profile",
    )
    bio = models.TextField()
    def __str__(self):
        return f"Profile for {self.user}"
```

This structure gives us a clean extension model for user-specific information. We can now access a profile through **user.profile**, which keeps our code expressive and easy to read. That single line of reverse navigation is one of the reasons relationship design matters so much in Django.

'ForeignKey' Relationships

A **ForeignKey** defines a many-to-one relationship, which means many records in one model can point to a single record in another model. This is one of the most common relationships we will use in everyday Django development. In our project, a single user can create many snippets, but each snippet should belong to one author. It makes ownership clear and keeps our data model easy to query. We will again use **settings.AUTH_USER_MODEL** and a **related_name** because we want reverse access from the user side to read naturally when we work through query examples and later recipes.

```
from django.conf import settings
from django.db import models
class Snippet(models.Model):
    author = models.ForeignKey(
        settings.AUTH_USER_MODEL,
        on_delete=models.CASCADE,
```

```
        related_name="snippets",
    )
    title = models.CharField(max_length=100)
    code = models.TextField()
    def __str__(self):
        return self.title
```

This relationship now moves us in both directions. We can fetch the author from a snippet with snippet.author, and we can fetch all snippets for a user with **`user.snippets.all()`**. It is the sort of navigation that makes Django's ORM feel productive once the models are shaped well.

Many-to-Many Relationships

A **`ManyToManyField`** is useful when instances on both sides of a relationship can connect to many instances on the other side. The tags are a classic example because one snippet can have many tags, and one tag can describe many snippets. We want the relationship to feel natural from the snippet side because that is where we will likely spend most of our time in GitforGits. For that reason, it is clearer to place the field on the Snippet model and let the reverse relation live on tag through **`related_name`**.

```
from django.db import models
class Tag(models.Model):
    name = models.CharField(max_length=30, unique=True)
    def __str__(self):
        return self.name
class Snippet(models.Model):
    author = models.ForeignKey(
        settings.AUTH_USER_MODEL,
        on_delete=models.CASCADE,
        related_name="snippets",
    )
    title = models.CharField(max_length=100)
    code = models.TextField()
```

```
    tags = models.ManyToManyField(Tag,
related_name="snippets", blank=True)

    def __str__(self):

        return self.title
```

This above model arrangement gives us several useful paths immediately. We can ask for **snippet.tags.all()** when we want every tag attached to one snippet, and we can ask for **tag.snippets.all()** when we want every snippet that shares a particular tag. Since many-to-many relationships involve multiple rows in a separate intermediary table, this is also the relationship type where **prefetch_related**("tags") becomes especially valuable. That tells Django to gather related tags efficiently rather than generating a fresh query every time we touch the tags attribute while looping through snippets.

'GenericForeignKey' Relationships

A **GenericForeignKey** is useful when one model must point to more than one type of target model. We should use it carefully, but it is extremely helpful in the right situation. The comments are a good example because we may want a single comment model to attach itself to snippets, profiles, or other content in the future without creating a different comment model for each one. This relationship relies on Django's content types framework. We store the model type in one field, the object's primary key in another field, and then expose them together as a single logical relationship through **content_object**.

```
from django.contrib.contenttypes.fields import
GenericForeignKey

from django.contrib.contenttypes.models import ContentType

from django.db import models

class Comment(models.Model):

    content_type = models.ForeignKey(ContentType,
on_delete=models.CASCADE)

    object_id = models.PositiveBigIntegerField()

    content_object = GenericForeignKey("content_type",
"object_id")

    text = models.TextField()

    class Meta:

        indexes = [
```

```
            models.Index(fields=["content_type",
"object_id"]),
        ]
    def __str__(self):
        return self.text[:50]
```

This above model gives us a flexible comment system that can follow our application.

After defining all such models, we should create and run migrations through shell or admin. From there, querying becomes very natural wherein we can use **select_related**("author") for the author relationship, **prefetch_related**("tags") for tags, and **content-type-aware** lookups for generic comments.

Recipe 2: Modeling Composite Primary Keys

There are times when a single auto-generated identifier is not the most natural way to describe the identity of a row. Some tables are defined more accurately by a combination of fields. In GitforGits, we may store the membership of snippets inside collections, and the true identity of that row may be the pair formed by the collection and the snippet. One collection can contain many snippets, and one snippet can belong to many collections, but the same snippet should not appear twice in the same collection. So here, a composite primary key is a good fit for this kind of modeling because the identity is not artificial. The identity comes directly from the business rule.

Defining Composite Primary Key

We already have collections that group snippets together. So now, we can create a junction model named **CollectionSnippet** to represent the placement of a snippet inside a collection. Instead of adding a separate surrogate id field, we can use the combination of **collection_id** and **snippet_id** as the primary key. It gives the table a very direct and meaningful identity. We will also keep an **added_at** timestamp so we know when the relationship was created.

```
from django.db import models
class Collection(models.Model):
    name = models.CharField(max_length=100)
    def __str__(self):
        return self.name
class CollectionSnippet(models.Model):
```

```
    pk = models.CompositePrimaryKey("collection_id",
"snippet_id")
    collection = models.ForeignKey(Collection,
on_delete=models.CASCADE)
    snippet = models.ForeignKey("Snippet",
on_delete=models.CASCADE)
    added_at = models.DateTimeField(auto_now_add=True)
```

The above structure makes our intent very clear. The pair of foreign keys is the identity of the row. That means the same snippet cannot appear twice in the same collection unless we redesign the model deliberately. It also means our primary key is no longer a single integer-like value. The **pk** attribute behaves as a tuple, and that is an important mental shift when we write query code, debugging output, serializers, or any helper logic that assumes a primary key is always one scalar value.

Querying Composite Key Models

The next step is to understand how we interact with the model. Since the primary key is made from two fields, the Django expects that identity to be represented as a tuple when we query by **pk**.

We do not need special query methods for ordinary lookups. We simply need to remember that the identity is made of two parts. We are teaching ourselves how the ORM will behave once the model is live and carrying data.

```
collection_snippet = CollectionSnippet.objects.get(
    pk=(collection.id, snippet.id)
)
matches = CollectionSnippet.objects.filter(
    pk=(collection.id, snippet.id)
)
```

We can also query through the constituent fields directly, and in many cases that reads even more clearly in business logic. For example, if we are checking whether a snippet already belongs to a collection, filtering by collection and snippet together may feel more explicit than using the **pk** tuple. Both styles are useful.

Migration and Design Considerations

A composite primary key deserves a little more care at design time than an ordinary surrogate key.

We should think through that choice before the model becomes deeply woven into the rest of the application. A model like **CollectionSnippet** works well because the row naturally represents the pairing of two objects.

We should also remember that composite key models are not the best fit for every situation. When a table needs to be referenced broadly by other models, or when the surrounding tools assume a single-column key, a regular auto field plus a uniqueness constraint may still be the simpler path.

```
python manage.py makemigrations
python manage.py migrate
```

Once the migrations are applied, we should test the model in the shell and verify that duplicate pairings are not allowed. We should also think about how forms, admin workflows, and related models will interact with this design before we commit heavily to it in a larger application.

The point of this recipe is not to force composite keys everywhere. The point is to recognize when they express the data more honestly and use them with intention.

Recipe 3: Working with Custom Managers and QuerySets

The improvements in database interactions with models is must for efficient and clean code. Although Django's ORM is very powerful, there are instances when we may desire additional control or a way to simplify frequent queries on our models. So here in this recipe, we use QuerySets and custom managers. To improve the interaction with the models we defined earlier, this recipe will teach us the creation of custom managers and QuerySets.

Defining Custom Queryset

For this recipe, we will continue to work with a **Snippet** model from the previous recipe. We will start by defining a custom QuerySet in our **models.py**:

```
from django.db import models
class SnippetQuerySet(models.QuerySet):
 def featured(self):
 return self.filter(is_featured=True)
 def by_language(self, language):
 return self.filter(language=language)
 def short_snippets(self, max_length=100):
```

```
return self.filter(length__lte=max_length)
```

This above custom QuerySet, **SnippetQuerySet**, provides three methods, like **featured()**, **by_language()**, and **short_snippets()**, and each of them are encapsulating a specific query.

Creating Custom Manager

The Django models come with a default manager named **objects**. It is the gateway to Django's database query operations.

In the following, we will integrate the **SnippetQuerySet** with a custom manager to make these methods accessible through the manager:

```
class SnippetManager(models.Manager):
 def get_queryset(self):
 return SnippetQuerySet(self.model, using=self._db)
 def featured(self):
 return self.get_queryset().featured()
 def by_language(self, language):
 return self.get_queryset().by_language(language)
 def short_snippets(self, max_length=100):
 return self.get_queryset().short_snippets(max_length)
```

In the above, the **SnippetManager** overrides the **get_queryset()** method to return instances of our custom QuerySet. It also provides convenience methods to directly access the custom QuerySet methods.

Attaching Custom Manager to Model

Finally, we will apply this custom manager to our **Snippet** model:

```
class Snippet(models.Model):
 # model fields go here
 objects = SnippetManager()
```

Here, we are replacing the default manager with our custom one, and the custom QuerySet methods turns accessible through **Snippet.objects**. With this, we can now easily retrieve model instances using the defined methods, and it therefore makes our model interactions more expressive. For instance, to get all featured snippets, we can simply use **Snippet.objects.featured()**.This particular approach centralizes the query logic within the model layer, and it quite adheres to Django's DRY principle.

Recipe 4: Implementing Soft Deletion in Models

There may be times when we should not remove records from the database irretrievably. There is an alternate way like we rather mark them as deleted so the data remains intact for future use in analysis, recovery, or record-keeping.

With Django's soft deletion feature, we can hide "deleted" records from regular queries but still access them when needed. It requires a different way of thinking about model definition and querying.

Extending Model for Soft Deletion

To implement soft deletion, we can add a **is_deleted** field to our models, which will indicate whether a record is considered deleted. For the **Snippet** model, the modification would look like this:

```
from django.db import models
class Snippet(models.Model):
 title = models.CharField(max_length=100)
 code = models.TextField()
 language = models.CharField(max_length=50)
 created_at = models.DateTimeField(auto_now_add=True)
 is_deleted = models.BooleanField(default=False)
 def delete(self, *args, **kwargs):
 self.is_deleted = True
 self.save()
 def __str__(self):
 return self.title
```

In this case, the **delete** method is overridden to set the **is_deleted** flag to **True** instead of actually deleting the record from the database.

Excluding Soft Deleted Records

To ensure that soft-deleted records are not included in query results by default, we can define a custom manager for the model:

```
class SnippetManager(models.Manager):
 def get_queryset(self):
 return super().get_queryset().filter(is_deleted=False)
class Snippet(models.Model):
 # Model fields as defined previously...
 objects = SnippetManager()
```

This custom manager overrides the **get_queryset** method to filter out records where **is_deleted** is **True**.

Retrieving Soft Deleted Records

If we need to access soft-deleted records (for example, in an admin interface or for data recovery purposes), we can add another manager that includes these records:

```
class AllSnippetsManager(models.Manager):
 def get_queryset(self):
 return super().get_queryset()
class Snippet(models.Model):
 # Model fields and the default manager as defined
previously...
 all_objects = AllSnippetsManager()
```

In the above, **Snippet.objects.all()** will return only non-deleted records, while **Snippet.all_objects.all()** will include both deleted and non-deleted records.

There is no permanent removal of records from our database when we use soft deletion, which gives us more control over our data. In addition to showing us to implement soft deletion in Django models, it also elaborated the flexibility of Django's ORM for modifying data handling to fit our application's needs.

Recipe 5: Maintaining Data Integrity

In many of my projects, poor integrity rules quickly turns into duplicate snippet titles, invalid code entries, broken relationships, or partially completed writes that leave the database in an uncertain state.

Luckily, the Django gives us several layers of protection for this problem. There are some rules that belong at the field level, some belong at the model level, some belong in database constraints, and some belong in transactional operations that must succeed or fail together. If we apply those layers carefully, our models stop being passive containers and begin to act like reliable guardians of the application's data.

Field Rules, Choices, and Database Constraints

A good integrity strategy starts by making the model say as much as it can about valid data. Field types, blank, null, choices, uniqueness, and explicit constraints are not just convenience features. They are the first line of defense against bad data. For a Snippet model, we can express several useful rules directly in the model. The modern constraint system in Django is especially useful here because **`UniqueConstraint`** and **`CheckConstraint`** let us express business rules at the database level instead of relying only on form validation or view logic.

```
from django.conf import settings
from django.core.exceptions import ValidationError
from django.db import models
def validate_code(value):
    blocked_terms = ["subprocess", "os.system"]
    for term in blocked_terms:
        if term in value:
            raise ValidationError(f"Code cannot contain
{term}.")
class Snippet(models.Model):
    class Language(models.TextChoices):
        PYTHON = "PY", "Python"
        JAVASCRIPT = "JS", "JavaScript"
        HTML = "HTML", "HTML"
    author = models.ForeignKey(
        settings.AUTH_USER_MODEL,
        on_delete=models.CASCADE,
```

```
        related_name="snippets",
    )
    title = models.CharField(max_length=100)
    code = models.TextField(validators=[validate_code])
    language = models.CharField(max_length=10,
choices=Language.choices)
    created_at = models.DateTimeField(auto_now_add=True)
    class Meta:
        constraints = [
            models.UniqueConstraint(
                fields=["author", "title"],
                name="unique_snippet_title_per_author",
            ),
            models.CheckConstraint(
                condition=~models.Q(title=""),
                name="snippet_title_not_empty",
            ),
            models.CheckConstraint(
                condition=~models.Q(code=""),
                name="snippet_code_not_empty",
            ),
        ]
    def clean(self):
        if self.title.strip().lower() ==
self.language.lower():
            raise ValidationError(
                {"title": "Title should be more descriptive
than the language name alone."}
            )
    def __str__(self):
```

```
        return self.title
```

This above model actively protects the shape of the data. The title cannot be duplicated for the same author, empty strings are rejected at the database level for the key text fields, and a reusable validator blocks obviously dangerous patterns in the code body. The **clean()** method then adds a model-level rule that is best expressed in Python because it checks the relationship between fields rather than the validity of one field in isolation. This layered design allows us to keep simple rules simple only and reserve the custom logic for the cases that truly need it.

Validation Flow and Safe Writes

The Forms and **ModelForms** already run validation as part of their normal workflow, which means field validators, model validation, uniqueness checks, and constraints can all contribute to a safer submission path. If we create a model instance in plain Python and call **save()**, Django does not automatically run **full_clean()** for us. And, this is why service-layer code, shell scripts, import jobs, and custom management commands deserve extra discipline.

When we want model validation to run in those paths, we should call **full_clean()** before **save()**. It keeps non-form code honest and prevents the false assumption that every object created in Python has already passed through the same validation net as a browser form.

```
snippet = Snippet(
    author=request.user,
    title="Sorting a List",
    code="numbers = sorted([4, 1, 9])",
    language=Snippet.Language.PYTHON,
)
snippet.full_clean()
snippet.save()
```

This pattern is worth adopting whenever our model instances are created programmatically outside form handling. It gives us a predictable validation checkpoint and keeps our model rules meaningful across different entry points into the application. We should not hide everything inside **save()** itself unless we have a very specific reason, because overriding **save()** for blanket validation can become awkward in bulk operations and data-loading scenarios.

Transactions for Multi-Step Integrity

Some integrity problems do not live in a single row. They appear when several database operations must succeed together or fail together. That is where transactions become essential. If we create a snippet and then attach tags, we do not want the snippet row to remain in the database if tag assignment fails halfway through. A transaction gives us one protective envelope for that sequence, which means either the whole operation commits or the whole thing rolls back.

A clean transaction boundary often does more for data integrity than dozens of scattered conditionals because it treats a multi-step change as one unit of work.

```
from django.db import transaction

def create_snippet_with_tags(author, title, code, language,
tags):

    with transaction.atomic():

        snippet = Snippet(

            author=author,

            title=title,

            code=code,

            language=language,

        )

        snippet.full_clean()

        snippet.save()

        snippet.tags.add(*tags)

        return snippet
```

This recipe teaches us, that data integrity is a set of complementary habits. The field options shape the first layer, validators and **clean()** add reusable application rules, constraints protect the database itself, and transactions guard multi-step operations. Once we put those pieces together, our model layer becomes much harder to break accidentally. And, that is exactly what we want in a project to grow chapter after chapter.

Recipe 6: Integrating with PostgreSQL

Although SQLite is convenient when we are getting started, but PostgreSQL is going to be a stronger choice once we need concurrency, richer data capabilities, and a database engine that can scale comfortably with more demanding workloads.

So for our app, the most practical way to integrate it in our Django is to use the PostgreSQL backend together with **psycopg 3** and keep the connection settings driven by environment variables rather than hard-coding secrets into settings.py. It will give us a cleaner project structure, safer configuration management, and a setup that moves more naturally from local development into staging and production.

Installing 'psycopg 3'

For a local development environment, the psycopg[binary] is a practical choice because it gives us a working binary package quickly. For deployment environments, teams often move to a system-linked build, but the integration pattern inside Django remains the same. The important point for the recipe is that we now use the **psycopg 3** family rather than the older psycopg2 path.

```
python -m pip install "psycopg[binary]"
```

Once the driver is installed, we can prepare environment variables for the database connection. This is a better pattern than placing usernames, passwords, and hostnames directly in the settings file because it keeps sensitive information out of source control and makes it easier to run the same codebase against different databases in different environments.

```
export DB_NAME=gitforgitsdb
export DB_USER=gitforgitsuser
export DB_PASSWORD=strongpassword
export DB_HOST=127.0.0.1
export DB_PORT=5432
```

The values above are my some random example, but the overall shape is exactly what we want to carry whenever configuration belongs to the environment rather than the code itself.

Configuring Django with Environment-driven Settings

Next, we then update the **gitforgits/settings.py** so the **DATABASES** setting reads from the environment. We can also define a configurable **CONN_MAX_AGE** so we have a clear place to manage persistent connections if the deployment style needs them later.

```
from pathlib import Path
import os
BASE_DIR = Path(__file__).resolve().parent.parent
DATABASES = {
    "default": {
        "ENGINE": "django.db.backends.postgresql",
        "NAME": os.environ.get("DB_NAME", "gitforgitsdb"),
```

```
        "USER": os.environ.get("DB_USER", "gitforgitsuser"),
        "PASSWORD": os.environ.get("DB_PASSWORD", ""),
        "HOST": os.environ.get("DB_HOST", "127.0.0.1"),
        "PORT": os.environ.get("DB_PORT", "5432"),
        "CONN_MAX_AGE": int(os.environ.get("DB_CONN_MAX_AGE",
"0")),
    }
}
```

This above configuration is direct, readable, and practical. It removes secrets from the code, keeps the backend explicit, and gives us one place to manage database connection settings cleanly. If we later deploy the project in containers, on a platform service, or through a traditional server configuration, these same environment variables can be supplied from the deployment layer without changing the application code. That is one of the reasons environment-driven settings are such a good fit for Django projects.

Applying Migrations

With the configuration in place, we can move the schema into PostgreSQL by running migrations. And, after the migration finishes, we should verify the connection by using the shell or admin and confirming that reads and writes behave normally.

```
python manage.py migrate
python manage.py shell
Inside the shell, we can perform a quick smoke test:
from snippets.models import Snippet
Snippet.objects.count()
```

At this point, GitforGits is using PostgreSQL through **psycopg 3** with settings that can move cleanly across environments. That gives us a strong baseline for everything that follows in this chapter, especially integrity rules, indexing, and performance work.

Recipe 7: Using psycopg 3 and PostgreSQL Connection Pools

A PostgreSQL connection costs time to establish, and repeated open-close cycles can add unnecessary latency. And, this is where a connection pool becomes useful. A pool keeps a managed set of reusable connections available for the application. In Django, the pooling support for PostgreSQL is available when we use psycopg and install the pool package.

Installing Pool Support Package

The pool objects are distributed separately from the base psycopg package, so we need to add the pool extra before Django can use pooling through the database settings.

```
python -m pip install "psycopg[pool]"
```

Once this extra is installed, the Django can pass the pool settings into psycopg's connection pool implementation through the **OPTIONS** section of the database configuration. It keeps the feature close to the rest of our database settings instead of pushing it into custom bootstrap code or ad hoc helper modules.

Configuring Pool

We can now extend our existing **DATABASES** setting with a pool entry under **OPTIONS**. We will also keep those values environment-driven so they can be tuned without editing the code.

In an ASGI deployment, it is generally better to keep persistent connections disabled and let the pool manage connection reuse instead of combining a long-lived connection strategy with a pool.

```
export DB_POOL_MIN_SIZE=1
export DB_POOL_MAX_SIZE=10
export DB_POOL_TIMEOUT=10
import os
DATABASES = {
    "default": {
        "ENGINE": "django.db.backends.postgresql",
        "NAME": os.environ.get("DB_NAME", "gitforgitsdb"),
        "USER": os.environ.get("DB_USER", "gitforgitsuser"),
        "PASSWORD": os.environ.get("DB_PASSWORD", ""),
        "HOST": os.environ.get("DB_HOST", "127.0.0.1"),
        "PORT": os.environ.get("DB_PORT", "5432"),
        "CONN_MAX_AGE": 0,
        "OPTIONS": {
```

```
            "pool": {
                "min_size":
int(os.environ.get("DB_POOL_MIN_SIZE", "1")),
                "max_size":
int(os.environ.get("DB_POOL_MAX_SIZE", "10")),
                "timeout":
int(os.environ.get("DB_POOL_TIMEOUT", "10")),
            }
        },
    }
}
```

This above configuration allows us to tune the pool without editing the settings file. On a local machine, a small pool may be enough. However, in a staging or production environment, the maximum size may need to grow, but we still want it to be deliberate because database connections are not unlimited resources. A pool is valuable precisely because it helps us reuse connections rather than opening too many of them. It is not a magical speed switch, but it is one part of a healthy database strategy.

Using Pooling

A connection pool is most useful when the application performs enough database work for connection reuse to matter. That usually means environments with multiple concurrent requests, repeated short-lived database interactions, or enough overall traffic that connection churn becomes noticeable. For a tiny local demo, the difference may be small. For a live application, the benefit can be meaningful. So here, my best advice would be to treat pooling as part of the operational setup of the project and to size it deliberately according to the database server's capacity. And, this is why, the environment-driven values matter again. They let us adjust the pool to the needs of the deployment rather than pretending one fixed size fits every environment.

With this recipe, we now have a correct PostgreSQL setup, and also more ready for real workloads. And, we also have a **psycopg 3** integration, environment-driven configuration, and a pool that can reuse connections efficiently. That sets us up well for the next recipe, where we will try to focus on making the work done over those connections faster through better indexes and more careful query patterns.

Recipe 8: Implementing Index and Query Optimization

A feature might look fine in development, but once tables grow, relationships deepen and common screens start interacting with several models, it can feel sluggish. For GitforGits, that risk is very real because listing snippets, filtering by language, loading authors, and resolving tags can all produce extra database work if we leave the ORM on autopilot. Basically, good optimisation isn't about filling the database with indexes willy-nilly or turning every queryset into a confusing mess. It means understanding how we use the site, choosing the right indexes to match, and using Django's query tools in a way that keeps database work deliberate and efficient. And that's where you'll see real and lasting improvements in performance.

Adding Indexes for Real Query Patterns

An index is most useful when it supports the way we actually filter, sort, or join data. For our app, fields such as **author**, **language**, and **created_at** are strong candidates because we are likely to filter by author, browse by language, and order recent snippets frequently. The Django gives us two direct ways to express, such as **db_index=True** for simple cases and **Meta.indexes** for multi-column or functional indexes.

```
from django.conf import settings
from django.db import models
from django.db.models.functions import Lower
class Snippet(models.Model):
    author = models.ForeignKey(
        settings.AUTH_USER_MODEL,
        on_delete=models.CASCADE,
        related_name="snippets",
        db_index=True,
    )
    title = models.CharField(max_length=100)
    code = models.TextField()
    language = models.CharField(max_length=10, db_index=True)
    created_at = models.DateTimeField(auto_now_add=True)
    class Meta:
        indexes = [
            models.Index(
                fields=["author", "-created_at"],
```

```
            name="snippet_author_created_idx",
        ),
        models.Index(
            fields=["language", "-created_at"],
            name="snippet_language_created_idx",
        ),
        models.Index(
            Lower("title"),
            name="snippet_lower_title_idx",
        ),
    ]
```

This model gives us three practical index shapes. The first two speed up common filtering and ordering patterns, and the functional index on Lower("title") helps when we want case-insensitive title lookups that still have index support.

In addition, every insert, update, or delete involving indexed columns requires more work from the database. Hence, the best indexing strategy begins with observed query patterns and profiling. We should try to add indexes that match real usage, confirm they help, and resist the temptation to treat indexing as a universal cure.

Writing Querysets

The indexes help the database find rows faster, but queryset design still matters just as much because poor relationship loading can create waste even with good indexes in place. The Django gives us excellent tools here, like the **select_related()** works best for single-valued relationships such as **ForeignKey** and **OneToOneField**, while **prefetch_related()** works best for many-to-many and reverse relationships. Those two methods are often the difference between one well-planned set of queries and a noisy loop that quietly fires off dozens of extra lookups. We should also avoid retrieving columns we do not need when a page only shows a small subset of fields, and we should choose **exists()** or **count()** when we need a yes-or-no or a count rather than full model instances.

```
snippets = (
    Snippet.objects
    .select_related("author")
    .prefetch_related("tags")
```

```
    .only("id", "title", "language", "created_at",
"author__username")
    .order_by("-created_at")
)
python_snippets = (
    Snippet.objects
    .filter(language="PY")
    .select_related("author")
    .order_by("-created_at")
)
```

These above queryset patterns keep the intent readable while reducing wasted work. The first example prepares a snippet listing page that needs author information and tags, while the second focuses on a language-filtered listing that still benefits from loading the related author in the same query. The Django gives us enough power to write efficient queries without turning ordinary code into something cryptic.

Even at this stage, simple B-tree indexes, good constraints, and relationship-aware query loading do a great deal of work before we ever reach more specialized PostgreSQL features. When we later move into richer search or PostgreSQL-specific capabilities, the Django will give us access to advanced index classes and PostgreSQL-aware expressions, but those tools work best when our basics will be very strong.

Summary

To sum up, we explored how Django model's real-world relationships and how those relationships shaped and queried our data. We worked through one-to-one, foreign key, many-to-many, and generic relationships so we could model profiles, snippets, tags, and reusable comments with clarity. We also examined composite primary keys, and alongside that, we saw how custom managers and querysets helped us centralize common query logic and make our model interactions more expressive and maintainable.

Later, we then learned to react to model lifecycle events with signals, preserve recoverable records through soft deletion, and protect application data through validators, constraints, model checks, and transactions. After that, we integrated Django with PostgreSQL using psycopg 3, then extended setup with connection pools so database access could remain cleaner and more efficient under load. And lastly, we then studied indexing and query optimization, where we matched indexes to real access patterns and used ORM tools such as **`select_related()`**, **`prefetch_related()`**, and targeted field to reduce unnecessary database work and keep

GitforGits fast and dependable as its data grew.

CHAPTER 3: MASTERING DJANGO'S URL DISPATCHER AND VIEWS

Overview

This chapter will take us into one of the most active parts of Django development, which is the point where URLs, views, forms, and request handling begin to work together as the visible behavior of the application. We start with dynamic URL routing to capture values from incoming paths and pass them into views so that one route pattern can serve many different pages. After that, we will organize our route structure with app-level URL configurations and namespacing so the project will remain easier to grow and maintain as more features are added. We will then work with both class-based and function-based views so we can learn to support different styles of request handling.

Next, we will use Django's generic views to reduce repeated code for familiar application patterns such as listing objects and processing object creation forms. We will also move beyond individual views and learn to use middleware for applying logic across the full request and response cycle in a reusable way. After that, we will secure the application more carefully by using permission checks, custom user checks, and a broader login-by-default policy so that authenticated access can be enforced consistently across the project. By the end of the chapter, we understand Django's URL dispatcher, views, middleware, and access control tools to build applications that are structured clearly, respond cleanly to user actions, and remain secure.

Recipe 1: Implement Dynamic URL Routing

The web applications rely on dynamic URL routing when they need to serve many pages through a clean and adaptable URL structure. In GitforGits, we do not want to define a separate hard-coded route for every snippet or every profile. We want one well-shaped pattern that can capture a value from the URL and send that value into a view. That is what makes URL routing dynamic. Once we understand this pattern, we can build views for snippet pages, profile pages, filtered resources, and many other content-driven screens without duplicating route definitions. Our goal in this recipe is to capture a value from the URL, pass it into a view, and let Django resolve the correct object using that value.

Defining Dynamic URL Pattern

If you are not aware of, the Django allows us to capture typed values directly in a route by using path converters. For a snippet detail page, the most natural value to capture is the snippet's identifier, so we will define a route that expects integer and passes it into view as **`snippet_id`**.

```
from django.urls import path
from . import views
urlpatterns = [
```

```
    path("snippets/<int:snippet_id>/", views.snippet_detail,
name="snippet_detail"),
]
```

The route remains simple, and it teaches that, one path pattern can represent many pages as long as the variable part of the URL is captured and handed to the view correctly.

Creating View Function

Now we need a view that receives the captured value and uses it to retrieve the correct object. So here, a small refinement helps here like, instead of wrapping the lookup in a manual try and except block, we can use **get_object_or_404()** to keep the view shorter and express our intent more clearly. The view should attempt to fetch the snippet with the given primary key and return a simple response that confirms the correct object was found.

```
from django.http import HttpResponse
from django.shortcuts import get_object_or_404
from .models import Snippet
def snippet_detail(request, snippet_id):
    snippet = get_object_or_404(Snippet, pk=snippet_id)
    return HttpResponse(f"Viewing snippet: {snippet.title}")
```

The above maintains the focus of this solution on routing rather than on template rendering, which belongs more naturally to a later recipe in the chapter.

With the URL pattern and view in place, we can start the development server and navigate to a path such as **/snippets/1/**, assuming a snippet with primary key 1 exists. If it does, Django will capture the integer from the URL, call the view with **snippet_id=1**, retrieve the matching object, and return the response. It gives full end-to-end proof that the route, the converter, the view, and the model lookup all work together properly. Once this pattern is understood, we can reuse it again and again across the project to build flexible detail pages without multiplying static route definitions.

Recipe 2: Using Advanced URL Configurations and Namespacing

With time, the URL configuration of our project will grow. If every route for every app is placed directly in the project URL file, the structure becomes difficult to read and even harder to maintain. If our GitforGits benefits from modular URL configuration because snippets, collaboration, user accounts, and future app modules can each keep their own routes close to their own views. The namespacing adds another layer of clarity by preventing naming collisions and giving us a predictable way to reverse routes in templates and views.

So, in this recipe, we will learn to keep URLs app-focused, preserve readability, and make future growth easier to manage.

Including App-specific URLs

The Django gives us **include()** so the project-level URL configuration can delegate to app-level URL files. It is a simple idea, but it has a large payoff because it keeps each app responsible for its own public routes. In our app, the main project can hand over any path beginning with **snippets/** to the snippets app, and the app can then decide how the remaining path should be interpreted.

```
from django.urls import include, path
urlpatterns = [
    path("snippets/", include("snippets.urls")),
]
```

From the above, it means our project URL file remains short and our app URL file remains focused on the app's own features rather than on the whole site.

Applying Namespacing

After having own URL file, we can give it a namespace by defining **app_name**. It is useful when more than one app may contain routes with names such as detail, create, or list. The namespace enable us distinguish them clearly. We will continue the same snippet detail example and keep the route compact, but we will now make the reverse name explicit through the namespace. It gives us a stable and expressive URL vocabulary in both templates and Python code.

```
from django.urls import path
from . import views
app_name = "snippets"
urlpatterns = [
    path("<int:snippet_id>/", views.snippet_detail,
name="snippet_detail"),
]
```

In the template, we can reverse the route like this:

```
{% url "snippets:snippet_detail" snippet_id=snippet.id %}
```

Reversing Namespaced URLs in Views

The same namespaced route can be reversed in Python by using **reverse()**.

```
from django.urls import reverse

def my_view(request):

    detail_url = reverse("snippets:snippet_detail",
kwargs={"snippet_id": 1})

    # Use detail_url as needed...
```

The above is useful when we want to build links dynamically or redirect to named routes without hard-coding URL strings. It helps our code stay stable even if the actual route pattern changes later, because the rest of the application can continue referring to the route by name. It is one of the strongest reasons to use namespacing consistently.

This setup keeps URL management clean and app-focused while reducing the risk of collisions as the project expands. It also makes route usage easier to read because the app name becomes part of the route identity. That clarity pays off quickly in larger applications, especially once templates, redirects, and navigation patterns begin to grow.

Recipe 3: Handling Form Data with Class-based Views

Form handling is the most common job in a web app. The Django's class-based views give us a structured way to handle that work without repeating the same logic across multiple functions. A class-based view helps us organize that flow through attributes and methods instead of keeping every step in one function body.

In this recipe, We will learn implementing the class to display a form, validate submitted data, save the object, and redirect the user after success.

Creating Form

At first, we begin to define a **ModelForm** for the Snippet model. It gives Django a clear description of which fields should appear in the form and how submitted data should map back to the model. A **ModelForm** remains a strong choice here because it keeps the form definition close to the model while still giving us room to customize later if needed. For this recipe, we only need the title, code, and language fields, which keeps the example focused on the class-based view rather than on advanced form customization.

```
from django import forms
from .models import Snippet
class SnippetForm(forms.ModelForm):
    class Meta:
        model = Snippet
        fields = ["title", "code", "language"]
```

Implementing Class-based View

Next, we then define the template name, the form class, and the URL to redirect to after success. Then we override **form_valid()** so the form is saved when the submitted data passes validation.

```
from django.urls import reverse_lazy
from django.views.generic.edit import FormView
from .forms import SnippetForm
class SnippetCreateView(FormView):
    template_name = "snippets/snippet_form.html"
    form_class = SnippetForm
    success_url = reverse_lazy("snippets:snippet_list")
    def form_valid(self, form):
        form.save()
        return super().form_valid(form)
```

This above keeps the view direct and understandable while still showing the basic pattern of class-based form handling. It also prepares us well for the next generic views recipe, where Django will take on even more of the repetitive work for us.

Wiring View to URL and Render Form

Now we connect the class-based view to a route and create a simple template for the form. Here, we call the **as_view()**, and it turns the class into a callable that Django can use as a normal view. A CSRF token, rendered fields, and a submit button are enough to complete the workflow. Once we submit valid data, the Django saves the snippet and redirects us to the list page.

```
from django.urls import path
from .views import SnippetCreateView
urlpatterns = [
    path("create/", SnippetCreateView.as_view(),
name="snippet_create"),
]
<h2>Add New Snippet</h2>
<form method="post">
    {% csrf_token %}
    {{ form.as_p }}
    <button type="submit">Submit</button>
</form>
```

The above gives compact but a complete example of class-based form handling in action.

This approach gives us a clear separation between configuration and behavior. The class attributes declare what the view uses, and the method override adds the one custom action we need. That balance is what makes class-based views attractive for recurring application patterns.

Recipe 4: Handling Form Data with Function-based Views

The function-based views remain valuable because they give us very direct control over request handling. For simpler form workflows, many developers prefer them because every step of the logic is visible in one place. In our app, a function-based view for creating a snippet is still a practical example because it enable us process **GET** and **POST** requests without introducing class structure where it may not yet feel necessary.

So here in this recipe, we will learn to handle form display and submission with a plain Python function while keeping the code easy to read and easy to reason about.

Reusing Form Definition

The form itself does not need to change just because the view style changes. We can keep the same **SnippetForm** and use it in a function-based view. It is one of the strengths of Django's forms system.

```
from django import forms
from .models import Snippet
class SnippetForm(forms.ModelForm):
    class Meta:
        model = Snippet
        fields = ["title", "code", "language"]
```

The form describes validation and field mapping once, and the view decides how to use it.

Processing GET and POST Requests

When the request method is **POST**, we bind the submitted data to the form, validate it, and save the snippet if the data is valid. When the request method is not **POST**, we create an empty form and display it. This style is still perfectly appropriate for small or medium-sized workflows because every branch of the logic is visible in one place. We do not need to jump between class attributes and methods to understand the flow.

```
from django.shortcuts import redirect, render
from .forms import SnippetForm
def create_snippet(request):
    if request.method == "POST":
        form = SnippetForm(request.POST)
        if form.is_valid():
            form.save()
            return redirect("snippets:snippet_list")
    else:
        form = SnippetForm()
    return render(request, "snippets/snippet_form.html",
{"form": form})
```

This is why function-based views continue to be useful even when Django offers many class-based alternatives.

Attaching View to Route

Next, we point a path at the view function and reuse the same template as the class-based example.

```
from django.urls import path
from .views import create_snippet
urlpatterns = [
    path("create/", create_snippet, name="snippet_create"),
]
<h2>Add New Snippet</h2>
<form method="post">
    {% csrf_token %}
    {{ form.as_p }}
    <button type="submit">Submit</button>
</form>
```

In the above, we can see clearly that Django does not force one single view style on us. It gives us a choice, and we can pick the one that fits the problem and our team's preferences best.

This function-based solution stays compact, readable, and completely valid for Django 6. It also keeps the form-handling flow easy to teach because we can follow the request from top to bottom without any hidden steps.

Recipe 5: Leveraging Django's Generic Views

Many web development tasks follow familiar patterns. We list objects, show details, create records, update records, and delete records. The Django's generic views exist to reduce the amount of repetitive code needed for those patterns while still giving us room to customize behavior when necessary.

Here, in this recipe, we will use Django's generic views to build common workflows with less code and clearer intent. Instead of writing the same structural logic again, we will allow Django to provide us the pattern and we supply the model, form, template, and redirect target.

Using Listview to Display Objects

A **`ListView`** is a natural fit when we want to display a collection of model instances. The Django can fetch the queryset, attach it to the template context, and render the template with very little code from us. We only need to define which model the view works with, which template should render the output, and what context name we want to use inside the template. It keeps the view small without making it mysterious. The configuration says exactly what the page is meant to do.

```
from django.views.generic import ListView
from .models import Snippet
class SnippetListView(ListView):
    model = Snippet
    template_name = "snippets/snippet_list.html"
    context_object_name = "snippets"
```

Using Createview to Handle Object Creation

A **CreateView** takes the repetitive work of displaying a form, validating submitted data, saving the model instance, and redirecting after success. Since this is a model-backed form flow, **CreateView** fits the problem especially well. We define the model, the form class, the template, and the success URL, and Django handles the rest of the standard workflow.

```
from django.urls import reverse_lazy
from django.views.generic.edit import CreateView
from .forms import SnippetForm
from .models import Snippet
class SnippetCreateView(CreateView):
    model = Snippet
    form_class = SnippetForm
    template_name = "snippets/snippet_form.html"
    success_url = reverse_lazy("snippets:snippet_list")
```

This is a good example of generic views at their best. They remove routine plumbing without hiding the important parts of the feature from us.

Connecting Generic Views to URLs

The final step is to connect the views to routes. One path can point to the list page and another can point to the creation page. It gives complete working example of two very common application patterns implemented with minimal code.

```
from django.urls import path
from .views import SnippetCreateView, SnippetListView
```

```
urlpatterns = [
    path("", SnippetListView.as_view(), name="snippet_list"),
    path("create/", SnippetCreateView.as_view(),
name="snippet_create"),
]
```

The real value of this recipe is not that it saves a few lines. It is the intent of each view, that becomes obvious from the class we choose. A **ListView** lists. A **CreateView** creates. It makes the codebase easier to navigate. Here, we still control the model, form, template, and redirects, but we avoid rewriting the same structural code again and again.

Recipe 6: Creating Custom Middleware for Request Processing

A Django application often needs behavior that should run for many requests rather than being repeated inside individual views. That is where middleware becomes useful. In GitforGits, we may want to add request metadata to responses, record who is accessing protected areas, or attach information that helps us understand how the application behaves in real use. The Middleware gives us a clean place to do that because it sits in the request and response path for the whole application.

In this recipe, we will learn to create a custom middleware class that processes requests in a reusable way.

Creating Middleware

So here, we will create a small middleware class that adds useful request metadata to the response. We will use the standard class pattern with **__init__()** and **__call__()**. Since GitforGits already has user-owned content such as snippets, it is useful for our middleware to recognize whether the request came from an authenticated user and, when it did, surface a small amount of safe metadata in response headers.

```
from django.utils.timezone import now
class RequestAuditMiddleware:
    def __init__(self, get_response):
        self.get_response = get_response
    def __call__(self, request):
        started_at = now()
```

```
        response = self.get_response(request)
        duration_ms = int((now() - started_at).total_seconds()
* 1000)
        response["X-Request-Duration-MS"] = str(duration_ms)
        if request.user.is_authenticated:
            response["X-Request-User"] =
request.user.get_username()
            response["X-Auth-Status"] = "authenticated"
        else:
            response["X-Auth-Status"] = "anonymous"
        return response
```

The important design detail is that middleware which depends on **request.user** must run after **AuthenticationMiddleware**, because that is the middleware that attaches the authenticated user object to the request. When a project also enables app-wide authentication, **LoginRequiredMiddleware** should come after **AuthenticationMiddleware**, and any middleware that is meant to observe or decorate already-authorized traffic should come after that login gate as well.

This middleware does three useful things:

- It measures how long the request took,
- It marks whether the request came from an authenticated user, and
- It adds the username for authenticated requests.

It also keeps the view layer focused on business behavior rather than application-wide plumbing. If we want it to observe requests after the application has already applied the login gate, we register it after both **AuthenticationMiddleware** and **LoginRequiredMiddleware**. That way, the middleware works with a populated **request.user** and mainly sees requests that have already passed the broad authentication rule or have been explicitly left public.

Registering Middleware in Login-aware Order

Now we activate the middleware in **settings.py**. The sessions must be available before authentication runs, authentication must run before a login gate can inspect request.user, and a custom middleware that wants to work with authenticated traffic should be positioned after those layers.

```
MIDDLEWARE = [
    "django.middleware.security.SecurityMiddleware",
```

```
    "django.contrib.sessions.middleware.SessionMiddleware",
    "django.middleware.common.CommonMiddleware",
    "django.middleware.csrf.CsrfViewMiddleware",
    "django.contrib.auth.middleware.AuthenticationMiddleware",
    "django.contrib.auth.middleware.LoginRequiredMiddleware",
    "snippets.middleware.RequestAuditMiddleware",
    "django.contrib.messages.middleware.MessageMiddleware",
    "django.middleware.clickjacking.XFrameOptionsMiddleware",
]
```

This ordering turns middleware into a sequence of responsibilities instead of a random list of components. It is the key thing we want to teach here, because middleware becomes much easier to reason about when we understand not only what each class does, but also what it expects to already exist on the request by the time it runs.

After adding the middleware, we can run the development server and inspect response headers. We should see the timing header on each response, and we should see authentication-related headers change depending on whether the current user is signed in. Once we understand that application-wide request handling can sit in middleware, it becomes much easier to understand why authentication can also be enforced broadly there, while view-level checks can focus on finer-grained permission and ownership rules.

Recipe 7: Securing Views with Permissions and User Checks

With time, not every authenticated user should be able to do everything. Some views should require ordinary login, some should require model permissions such as the ability to change snippets, and some should allow access only when a business rule is true, such as the current user being the author of the snippet or a staff reviewer. Authentication tells us who the user is. Authorization tells us what that user is allowed to do. Once a project begins using a login-by-default policy, we do not need to repeat basic login protection on every view.

So, in this recipe, we will keep those layers clear so our views remain readable, our access rules remain explicit, and our application stays safe with more roles and actions being added.

Using Permission Decorators for Function-based Views

For function-based views, the **`permission_required()`** remains a clean way to protect operations such as editing a snippet. When the application uses a login-by-default middleware, anonymous users are already redirected before they reach most protected views, so the view-level decorator can focus on authorization. In practical terms, that means we can use **permission_required(..., raise_exception=True)** to produce a 403 response for authenticated users who are signed in but still do not have the necessary permission. That is usually the behavior we want because it clearly distinguishes "please sign in" from "you are signed in but not allowed to do this." We can then add a second check for ownership or staff status when the business rule is narrower than the model permission alone.

```
from django.contrib.auth.decorators import permission_required
from django.core.exceptions import PermissionDenied
from django.shortcuts import get_object_or_404, render
from .models import Snippet
@permission_required("snippets.change_snippet",
raise_exception=True)
def edit_snippet(request, snippet_id):
    snippet = get_object_or_404(Snippet, pk=snippet_id)
    if snippet.author_id != request.user.id and not
request.user.is_staff:
        raise PermissionDenied("You do not have access to edit
this snippet.")
    if request.method == "POST":
        # Process the form here
        ...
    else:
        # Display the form here
        ...
    return render(request, "snippets/snippet_edit.html",
{"snippet": snippet})
```

This pattern keeps the view honest and readable. We do not pretend that a single permission always captures the full business rule. We acknowledge that a model permission such as **change_snippet** may still need to be paired with an ownership rule. It is also useful to remember that if we are not using app-wide login enforcement, we can still combine **login_required** and **permission_required** in a standalone view.

In a login-by-default project, however, the decorator above is usually enough for the authentication layer, and that enable the body of the view stay focused on who may act on this particular object and under what conditions.

Using Mixins and User Checks for Class-based Views

For class-based views, the **PermissionRequiredMixin** gives the same broad permission check in a form that matches Django's generic and object views nicely. Since the application may already require login globally, we often do not need to add **LoginRequiredMixin** to every class-based view. The middleware already covers that responsibility. The class can then concentrate on permissions and view behavior.

And, when we need business-specific checks, such as "the user must be the author or a staff member," overriding **dispatch()** or **get_object()** is often the clearest place to apply that rule.

```
from django.contrib.auth.mixins import PermissionRequiredMixin
from django.core.exceptions import PermissionDenied
from django.views.generic import UpdateView
from .forms import SnippetForm
from .models import Snippet
class EditSnippetView(PermissionRequiredMixin, UpdateView):
    model = Snippet
    form_class = SnippetForm
    template_name = "snippets/snippet_edit.html"
    permission_required = "snippets.change_snippet"
    pk_url_kwarg = "snippet_id"
    def dispatch(self, request, *args, **kwargs):
        snippet = self.get_object()
        if snippet.author_id != request.user.id and not
request.user.is_staff:
            raise PermissionDenied("You do not have access to
edit this snippet.")
        return super().dispatch(request, *args, **kwargs)
```

Here, the application-wide login gate controls whether the user reaches the view at all. The mixin checks for the required permission. The custom dispatch logic checks the specific ownership rule for the object being edited. Each of the layer solves a different problem, and because the responsibilities are separated cleanly, the code remains understandable.

Recipe 8: Enforcing Login By-Default

Many applications begin with individual **@login_required** decorators scattered across private views. That works for a while, but it becomes easy to miss a new route as the project turns complex and big. One forgotten decorator can quietly expose a screen that was meant to stay private.

For such an issue, a login-by-default strategy solves the problem by moving broad authentication rule into middleware. In it, the application treats views as protected unless we explicitly mark them as public. In our app, only a small set of endpoints, such as the landing page, sign-in page, sign-up page, and perhaps a public snippet showcase, should remain open by design. In this recipe, we will learn to add an app-wide authentication gate and then opt out only where public access is truly intended.

Enabling Login By-default

The first step is to add **LoginRequiredMiddleware** to MIDDLEWARE after **AuthenticationMiddleware**. This ordering matters because the login gate needs **request.user** to already exist. We should also define a **LOGIN_URL** so Django knows where to send unauthenticated users, and it is helpful to set **LOGIN_REDIRECT_URL** for the place users should land after a successful sign-in. Once this middleware is active, the application assumes that views require authentication unless we explicitly state otherwise.

```
MIDDLEWARE = [
    "django.middleware.security.SecurityMiddleware",
    "django.contrib.sessions.middleware.SessionMiddleware",
    "django.middleware.common.CommonMiddleware",
    "django.middleware.csrf.CsrfViewMiddleware",
    "django.contrib.auth.middleware.AuthenticationMiddleware",
    "django.contrib.auth.middleware.LoginRequiredMiddleware",
    "django.contrib.messages.middleware.MessageMiddleware",
    "django.middleware.clickjacking.XFrameOptionsMiddleware",
]
LOGIN_URL = "/accounts/login/"
```

```
LOGIN_REDIRECT_URL = "/snippets/"
```

This above will give us a secure default and removes the need to decorate every private view individually just to enforce ordinary login. It also changes how we think about view code. Once authentication is handled broadly, many views can focus on authorization and business rules instead of repeating the same sign-in requirement.

Opting Out for Public Endpoints

A login-by-default policy only works well if we have a clean way to declare that certain endpoints are intentionally public. That is where **login_not_required()** comes in. We can apply it to function-based views directly, and for class-based views, we can use **method_decorator()** on **dispatch()**. We are just marking the public endpoints in code.

```
from django.contrib.auth.decorators import login_not_required
from django.shortcuts import render
@login_not_required
def home(request):
    return render(request, "core/home.html")
from django.contrib.auth.decorators import login_not_required
from django.utils.decorators import method_decorator
from django.views.generic import TemplateView
@method_decorator(login_not_required, name="dispatch")
class PublicSnippetShowcaseView(TemplateView):
    template_name = "snippets/public_showcase.html"
```

From the above, we get a very strong application-wide access pattern. The middleware establishes the default rule, and the decorator marks the exceptions. Once this pattern is in place, the previous security recipe becomes easier to apply as well.

Summary

Overall, we explored how Django's URL dispatcher and view system shaped the way a web application received requests, identified the correct destination, and returned a meaningful response. We worked with dynamic URL routing so that values could be captured directly from the URL and passed into views for object lookup and page rendering. After that, we organized URLs more cleanly by using app-level URL configurations and namespacing, which made route management clearer and reduced the risk of collisions as the project structure became larger. We then handled form data with both class-based and function-based views for processing user input.

We also made use of Django's generic views to reduce repetitive code for common patterns such as listing objects and creating new ones. Next, we moved into request-wide processing through middleware to add reusable logic that could observe or modify requests and responses. We then strengthened the security story of the project by applying permission checks and custom user checks inside protected views. Finally, we expanded that protection with a login-by-default pattern, which allowed the application to treat most views as private unless they were intentionally marked as public.

Chapter 4: Templates, Static Files, and Media Management

Overview

This chapter will focus on the presentation layer that users interact with, through templates, assets, and rendered content. We begin with advanced template inheritance to create a stable application layout. We will use custom filters to shape how values are displayed and then move into reusable template partials so repeated interface fragments can be defined once and rendered in multiple places without duplication.

After that, we will learn to handle static files and user-uploaded media through a clearer storage configuration. We will also see how custom template tags will support dynamic content generation, how fragment caching will improve performance when applied carefully, and how the querystring tag will preserve filter and pagination state during navigation. Toward the end of the chapter, we will turn our attention to template loading efficiency so we can understand how loader configuration, inheritance depth, and fragment reuse will affect rendering speed.

Recipe 1: Creating Advanced Template Inheritance and Filters

Sometimes, a Django app may quickly run into a familiar presentation problem. We want every page to share the same visual identity, navigation, and structural rhythm, but we also need enough flexibility to shape each page around its own purpose. A snippet listing page, a snippet detail page, and a profile page should all feel like they belong to the same application, yet none of them should be forced into a rigid template that makes customization painful. This is where advanced template inheritance becomes important.

A strong base template gives us one place for shared layout, while carefully chosen blocks let child templates replace only what needs to change. At the same time, the filters allow us keep formatting logic close to the presentation layer without pushing tiny display transformations back into every view. In this recipe, we will reuse HTML and build a template structure that remains readable, adaptable, and easy to extend as our app adds more screens and more repeated interface fragments.

Designing Base Template

A useful base template should do more than hold a page title and one content block. It should define the stable frame of the application and offer named extension points that match the way pages actually vary. In our app, those extension points often include the page title, extra metadata in the **<head>**, the navigation area, the main content region, and a smaller section for contextual actions or sidebar content. When we shape the base template around those real needs, child templates become easier to read because they override meaningful blocks rather than fighting a layout that was too narrow from the beginning.

Following is a good base template which gives us consistency without turning every page into a compromise between what the layout expects and what the page actually needs.

```
<!DOCTYPE html>
<html lang="en">
<head>
    <meta charset="UTF-8">
    <title>{% block title %}GitforGits{% endblock %}</title>
    {% block meta %}{% endblock %}
</head>
<body>
    <header>
        <h1>GitforGits</h1>
        <nav>
            <a href="/">Home</a>
            <a href="/snippets/">Snippets</a>
            <a href="/profiles/">Profiles</a>
        </nav>
    </header>
    <main>
        <section class="page-content">
            {% block content %}
            <p>Default page content.</p>
            {% endblock %}
        </section>
        <aside class="page-aside">
            {% block aside %}
            <p>No additional actions for this page.</p>
            {% endblock %}
        </aside>
```

```
    </main>
    <footer>
        <p>Built with Django</p>
    </footer>
</body>
</html>
```

This above structure gives us one stable layout and several controlled points of variation. It is the right starting point for advanced inheritance because it teaches us to think in layers. The base template owns the overall page shell, while child templates own the page-specific content inside the slots we provide. This also makes later refactoring easier, because changes to shared navigation, footer markup, or wrapper structure can be made once in the base template instead of being repeated across every page template.

Extending Base Template with Page-specific Structure

Once the base template exists, a child template can focus on its own content instead of repeating the entire document structure. A snippet detail page, for example, can replace the title, define the main content, and optionally use the aside block for quick actions such as edit, delete, or related navigation. We should also notice that inheritance does not remove freedom. It channels it. A child template is still free to produce very different page content, but it does so within a stable application frame that keeps the interface coherent.

```
{% extends "base.html" %}
{% block title %}Snippet Details{% endblock %}
{% block content %}
<h2>{{ snippet.title }}</h2>
<p><strong>Language:</strong> {{ snippet.language }}</p>
<pre>{{ snippet.code }}</pre>
<p>Published on: {{ snippet.created_at|custom_date }}</p>
{% endblock %}
{% block aside %}
<h3>Snippet Actions</h3>
<a href="{% url 'snippets:snippet_edit' snippet.id
%}">Edit</a>
```

```
<a href="{% url 'snippets:snippet_delete' snippet.id
%}">Delete</a>
{% endblock %}
```

This child template stays compact because the base template has already taken responsibility for the page frame. That keeps our page-specific templates readable, which becomes more important as they grow richer. We also gain a natural place for display-oriented transformations such as the **custom_date** filter shown in the snippet output.

At this stage, it is helpful to think about the line between inheritance and reusable fragments.

Creating Custom Filters for Display Transformations

If we want dates to appear in one consistent house style, we can define a filter once and apply it wherever that style is needed. It keeps the templates expressive without pushing presentation details back into Python view logic over and over again. A filter should stay focused and transform a value for display, not perform broad business logic or expensive database work.

```
from django import template
register = template.Library()
@register.filter(name="custom_date")
def custom_date(value):
    return value.strftime("%Y-%m-%d at %H:%M")
```

Now, to use the filter, we will load its library and apply it where the value appears:

```
{% load your_custom_filters %}
<p>Published on: {{ snippet.created_at|custom_date }}</p>
```

Here, the view still prepares the data, the model still owns business state, and the template now has a simple way to present that data consistently. The filter does not replace inheritance, but it complements it well because both features reduce duplication in different directions.

When we combine them thoughtfully, our templates become easier to read because they describe both page structure and data presentation at the right level of abstraction.

Partial-aware Thinking for Repeated Fragments

A well-structured template system benefits from recognizing when repetition is happening at the fragment level rather than at the page level. A snippet metadata panel, a tag badge group, a flash message box, or a profile summary card may appear in several templates without being large enough to deserve another base template. This is the point where template partials become useful.

We do not need to force every repeated fragment into an {% include %} or copy the markup manually into multiple child templates. Instead, we can begin shaping our templates so repeated sections are easy to extract into named partials. In practice, that means writing fragment markup with clear input expectations, keeping the fragment's context clean, and avoiding hidden dependencies on variables that exist only in one template. This particular recipe introduced that way of thinking so our inheritance strategy does not stop at the page shell. It continued into the repeated pieces that live inside the page.

Recipe 2: Building Reusable Template Partials

At some point, a Django project will have the same markup in a bunch of templates. The snippet card can appear on the home page, the user dashboard, the snippet list and a search results page. There's a profile summary box that might pop up on the author page and the collaboration sidebar. It's fine copying those bits, but it makes maintenance harder because if you make one small design change, you have to apply it everywhere. This problem can be solved by using template partials, which let us define a named reusable fragment and render it wherever it's needed. It keeps repeated markup close to the template layer and helps us treat fragments as components without introducing a separate frontend framework.

In this recipe, we're going to use **{% partialdef %}** to define partials, then **{% partial %}** to render them, and finally use them to refactor repeated UI sections into templates that are cleaner and easier to maintain.

Defining Fragment as Named Partial

A template partial begins with a fragment that has a clear purpose and stable structure. In GitforGits, a snippet summary card is a strong candidate because it is small enough to reuse often and rich enough to justify centralizing. We will define that card once inside a template using **{% partialdef %}** and then render it with **{% partial %}** wherever we need it.

```
{% partialdef snippet_card %}
<article class="snippet-card">
    <h3>{{ snippet.title }}</h3>
    <p><strong>Language:</strong> {{ snippet.language }}</p>
    <p>{{ snippet.code|truncatechars:120 }}</p>
    <a href="{% url 'snippets:snippet_detail' snippet.id
%}">Read more</a>
</article>
{% endpartialdef %}
```

This above definition gives the fragment a name and a bounded purpose. The partial renders one card for one snippet, and that makes its behavior easy to understand. We are defining one reusable fragment that can appear in multiple places with the same basic shape.

Rendering Partial

Once the partial is defined, we can render it with **`{% partial %}`** wherever the current context already contains the right data. A list page is a perfect example because it often loops over snippets and repeats the same card structure. Instead of writing the same markup inline inside every loop, we can call the named partial and keep the loop itself very short.

```
{% extends "base.html" %}
{% block title %}All Snippets{% endblock %}
{% block content %}
<h2>All Snippets</h2>
{% partialdef snippet_card %}
<article class="snippet-card">
    <h3>{{ snippet.title }}</h3>
    <p><strong>Language:</strong> {{ snippet.language }}</p>
    <p>{{ snippet.code|truncatechars:120 }}</p>
    <a href="{% url 'snippets:snippet_detail' snippet.id
%}">Read more</a>
</article>
{% endpartialdef %}
<section class="snippet-grid">
    {% for snippet in snippets %}
        {% partial snippet_card %}
    {% empty %}
        <p>No snippets found.</p>
    {% endfor %}
</section>
{% endblock %}
```

This pattern keeps the page template readable because the repeated card markup now has a name and a home. That means if we later add a tag row, author line, or action button to the card, we update one fragment rather than hunting through multiple templates. The loop remains a loop, and the fragment remains a fragment.

Refactoring Repeated Fragments

The best way to adopt partials is to refactor repeated fragments that already exist, not to force partials into every template from day one. We should begin by scanning our templates for repeated blocks that are truly identical or very close to identical. A snippet preview card, a sidebar author box, or a small list item with metadata are all strong candidates. Once we find a repeated fragment, we move the shared markup into a named partial, make sure the required context variables are consistently available, and then replace each copied block with a `{% partial %}` call. It gives controlled refactor rather than a disruptive rewrite. We should keep the first few extractions simple so the project gains clarity immediately.

A useful rule for refactoring is that, if a fragment's markup repeats and its data expectations are stable, it belongs in a partial. If the repeated block only looks similar but actually needs different fields, actions, or layout assumptions in each place, we should leave it alone until the differences become clearer. This is why migration guidance matters. We do not want to treat every repeated `<div>` as a component. We want to extract fragments whose repeated purpose is already obvious and whose interface is small enough to stay understandable.

Combining Partials with Inheritance

Partials and inheritance work best together when each one handles the problem it was built for. Inheritance controls page-level structure. The partials control repeated inner fragments. That means a child template can extend base.html, override the main content block, and then use partials inside that block for repeated cards, alerts, or summary sections. This is the sweet spot for template reuse because each technique handles one layer of repetition without competing with the other.

A healthy partial strategy also improves team development. One developer can adjust a shared snippet card, while another works on page layout, without the two changes colliding in confusing ways. This recipe offers a practical component-like pattern inside Django templates. We define a repeated fragment once, render it where needed, and refactor duplicated markup into a cleaner, named unit. That keeps templates shorter, reduces maintenance cost, and makes repeated interface sections easier to evolve.

Recipe 3: Performing Efficient Static and Media Files Handling

A Django application serves two very different kinds of files, and many project problems begin when those two categories are treated as though they were the same thing. Static files are assets that belong to the application itself, such as CSS, JavaScript, icons, and images that we ship with the project. The media files are user-uploaded files, such as profile images, documents, or snippet attachments that are created after the application is already running. Static files are collected and deployed. The media files are stored and served as user content. Once we blur that distinction, configuration becomes messy, deployment becomes fragile, and security problems become more likely.

So here, this recipe make that boundary completely clear, configure Django's STORAGES setting properly, and build a file-handling structure that stays clean in development and remains predictable when the application moves into production.

Configuring Static and Media as Separate Storage

The first step is to make the settings reflect the fact that static and media files have different lifecycles. Static files belong to the codebase and are gathered with collectstatic. The media files belong to users and are written over time as the application runs. The Django's **STORAGES** setting gives us a clean way to describe those responsibilities explicitly. We still keep **STATIC_URL**, **STATIC_ROOT**, **MEDIA_URL**, and **MEDIA_ROOT**, but we now declare which storage handles default uploaded files and which storage handles collected static assets.

```
from pathlib import Path
BASE_DIR = Path(__file__).resolve().parent.parent
STATIC_URL = "/static/"
STATIC_ROOT = BASE_DIR / "staticfiles"
MEDIA_URL = "/media/"
MEDIA_ROOT = BASE_DIR / "media"
STORAGES = {
    "default": {
        "BACKEND":
"django.core.files.storage.FileSystemStorage",
    },
    "staticfiles": {
        "BACKEND":
"django.contrib.staticfiles.storage.StaticFilesStorage",
    },
}
```

```
STATICFILES_DIRS = [
    BASE_DIR / "static",
]
```

This configuration makes the difference between static and media explicit. The default storage is for uploaded files, while the staticfiles storage is for assets gathered by collectstatic. A local filesystem backend is perfectly fine here because this recipe's job is to teach the separation clearly before we move to more advanced deployment patterns.

Accessing files via Template Layer and Model Fields

The static files are part of our application design, so templates should reference them through the **{% static %}** tag. And, the media files, on the other hand, come from model fields such as **ImageField** and **FileField**, and templates should reference them through the stored file object's .url.

The static assets are resolved through the staticfiles system, while uploaded assets are resolved through the file field stored on the model. When we keep these access patterns distinct, our templates stay readable and our deployment story stays sane. We know immediately whether a file path belongs to the application bundle or to user content created later.

```
{% load static %}
<link rel="stylesheet" href="{% static 'css/site.css' %}">
<script src="{% static 'js/snippets.js' %}"></script>
{% if profile.avatar %}
    <img src="{{ profile.avatar.url }}" alt="{{
profile.user.username }}">
{% endif %}
```

This simple contrast does a lot of work for us. The stylesheet and script come from the application's static directory. The avatar comes from the user-uploaded media storage. Those two paths may both end in a browser-visible URL, but they should never be mentally grouped together as though they came from the same source.

Storing Uploaded files through Model Fields

A **FileField** or **ImageField** can use **upload_to** to keep uploads organized instead of dropping everything into one flat media directory. In our app, a profile avatar or snippet attachment is a good example because both are realistic uploads and both benefit from a predictable storage path. A clear upload path also makes backup, cleanup, and inspection easier because the files reflect the structure of the content they belong to. We can then render those files naturally through the model instance rather than building file paths manually.

```
from django.conf import settings
from django.db import models
class UserProfile(models.Model):
    user = models.OneToOneField(
        settings.AUTH_USER_MODEL,
        on_delete=models.CASCADE,
        related_name="profile",
    )
    avatar = models.ImageField(upload_to="avatars/",
blank=True, null=True)
class SnippetAttachment(models.Model):
    snippet = models.ForeignKey(
        "Snippet",
        on_delete=models.CASCADE,
        related_name="attachments",
    )
    file = models.FileField(upload_to="snippet_attachments/")
    uploaded_at = models.DateTimeField(auto_now_add=True)
```

It keeps the user content in media storage and powers the model carry the responsibility for where that content lives. We should avoid building upload paths directly in views or templates because that spreads storage assumptions across the application. A model field already knows how to manage its file, and we gain a much cleaner system when we let it do that job.

Serving Media and Deploying Static in Production

During development, the Django can help serve media files so we can see uploaded content without configuring a separate web server. Now, this is useful for local work, but it is a development convenience rather than the production plan.

The static files follow a different path. They should be collected into **STATIC_ROOT** with collectstatic so the deployment environment can serve them efficiently. This is why the separation between static and media matters operationally as well as conceptually. The static assets are gathered and published as part of deployment. The media files continue to arrive after deployment because users keep uploading them.

```
from django.conf import settings
from django.conf.urls.static import static
urlpatterns = [
    # Your URL patterns go here
]
if settings.DEBUG:
    urlpatterns += static(settings.MEDIA_URL,
document_root=settings.MEDIA_ROOT)
python manage.py collectstatic
```

This recipe gives us a clean and efficient mental model for file handling in Django. The static files belong to the application and are collected for deployment. And, the media files belong to users and are stored through the default file storage. The **STORAGES** makes those roles explicit, templates use the correct access pattern for each file type, and models define where uploaded files live.

Recipe 4: Creating Custom Template Tags for Dynamic Content

The built-in template tags and filters aren't going to cut it when our app gets more advanced. We will need to incorporate more sophisticated data manipulations into our templates. We might require a different way to show the most recent code snippets, real-time statistics aggregation, or even the ability to apply custom formatting to user-generated content.

So here, to begin with, we will create a module within our app to house these custom elements. For this, in our **snippets** app (or whichever app we are working on), we will create a directory named **templatetags**. The Django requires an **__init__.py** file inside this directory to recognize it as a valid Python module. And then, we create a Python file **snippet_tags.py** for our tags and filters.

Writing Custom Template Tag

To begin with, inside **snippet_tags.py**, we will write:

```
from django import template
```

```
from snippets.models import Snippet
register = template.Library()
@register.simple_tag
def get_latest_snippets(count=5):
 return Snippet.objects.order_by('-created_at')[:count]
```

This defines a simple tag called **get_latest_snippets** that returns the latest snippets. We can specify the number of snippets we want with the **count** parameter.

Using Custom Template Tag in Templates

To use this new tag, we first need to load the tag library with **{% load snippet_tags %}** at the top of our template file. And then, we can use our tag as follows:

```
{% load snippet_tags %}
<ul>
{% get_latest_snippets as latest_snippets %}
{% for snippet in latest_snippets %}
 <li>{{ snippet.title }}</li>
{% endfor %}
</ul>
```

This loads the **get_latest_snippets** tag, calls it to retrieve the latest snippets, and iterates over these snippets to display their titles. This method allows us to abstract complex logic into reusable components, and we can then keep our templates focused on presentation rather than data manipulation.

Recipe 5: Implementing Caching Strategies for Templates

Over period, the cost of rendering the same expensive template fragments again and again becomes easier to notice. Without caching, those fragments may trigger repeated queryset evaluation, repeated formatting, and repeated rendering work even when the visible output stays the same for long stretches of time. A cache is helpful only when the content inside it is stable for the duration of the cache entry. If we place highly dynamic or request-specific content inside the cached region, the cache can quietly serve stale or misleading output. This matters even more once a page uses request-specific security values such as CSP nonces.

So, in this recipe, we will learn to identify which template fragments are safe to cache, how to build stable cache keys, and how to avoid conflicts between fragment caching and per-request values that must remain fresh.

Choosing Fragment Caching

The fragment caching is usually a better fit because it enable us store only the section of the template that is expensive and relatively stable. A snippet metadata panel, a list of related snippets, or a statistics summary are all strong candidates if they do not change frequently and do not depend on volatile request-specific values. The Django's **{% cache %}** tag is well suited to this because it enable us define a cache lifetime and include one or more values that become part of the cache key. That gives us enough precision to store different fragment outputs for different snippets, pages, or filter states without accidentally collapsing them into one shared cached result.

```
{% load cache %}
{% cache 300 snippet_meta_panel snippet.id %}
<section class="snippet-meta">
    <h2>{{ snippet.title }}</h2>
    <p><strong>Language:</strong> {{ snippet.language }}</p>
    <p><strong>Author:</strong> {{ snippet.author.username
}}</p>
    <p><strong>Published:</strong> {{
snippet.created_at|date:"Y-m-d H:i" }}</p>
</section>
{% endcache %}
```

The most important discipline here is to cache the fragment whose rendered result is expensive, not to wrap large sections of the page just because doing so looks convenient. This fragment caches the snippet metadata for five minutes and uses the snippet's identifier as part of the cache key.

The gain here is not only speed. The gain is predictability. A useful rule is to read the cache tag as though it were a sentence. We are saying, "***cache this exact fragment for this exact object for this amount of time.***" Once the statement becomes vague, the cache boundary is probably too loose and should be tightened before we trust it in production.

Avoiding Nonce Values Cache Fragments

A fragment cache works by reusing rendered output, which means it can only remain correct when that output is supposed to be reusable across requests. A CSP nonce breaks that assumption because the nonce is request-specific. When a page uses inline **<script>** or **<style>** tags with a **nonce="{{ csp_nonce }}"** attribute, that nonce must match the nonce value inserted into the response's CSP header for the same request.

So here, a safer pattern is to cache the stable content itself, such as HTML data, and leave the nonce-bearing script or style tag uncached, or better yet, move the JavaScript or CSS to static files so the page does not depend on inline nonce-bearing blocks in the first place.

```
{% load cache %}
{% cache 300 snippet_body snippet.id %}
<section class="snippet-body">
    <h2>{{ snippet.title }}</h2>
    <pre>{{ snippet.code }}</pre>
</section>
{% endcache %}
<script nonce="{{ csp_nonce }}">
    window.snippetId = "{{ snippet.id }}";
</script>
```

This arrangement is much safer because the cached fragment contains only stable HTML, while the inline script remains request-specific and receives the correct nonce for the current response. The same principle applies to inline styles that carry a nonce.

Invalidating Caches

If a fragment changes whenever a snippet is edited, tagged, or reclassified, then the cache lifetime should reflect that reality. We can choose a short timeout for safety, or we can manually invalidate the relevant cache key when the underlying content changes. A short timeout is easier to manage when data changes often but can tolerate a brief delay. The explicit invalidation is stronger when freshness matters more and the relevant key is easy to compute. The main thing we should avoid is adding a cache and then forgetting that the application now has two states to think about. One is the database state and the other is the cached rendered state.

```
from django.core.cache import cache
def refresh_snippet_cache(snippet_id):
```

```
cache.delete(f"template.cache.snippet_meta_panel.{snippet_id}"
)
```

Good cache usage means we remain conscious of both. And, this is why fragment caching belongs next to template and data design rather than being treated as a separate performance trick. Once we understand what the fragment represents and how often its data changes, the cache decision becomes much easier to make and much less likely to produce stale or confusing pages.

This recipe illustrates the general idea, although the exact key strategy should stay aligned with the way the cache fragment is named and parameterized in the template. We should not cache a fragment merely because it exists. We should cache it because it is expensive enough, stable enough, and clearly bounded enough to benefit from reuse without confusing the user.

Recipe 6: Preserving Filters and Pagination using 'querystring'

A filtered list page becomes frustrating very quickly when each pagination click forgets the filters that produced the current result set. A user may choose a language, add a tag filter, sort by recency, and then click "next page," only to discover that the application has silently dropped the filter state and returned to a generic list. This is one of those small interface problems that makes an application feel less reliable than it actually is. The problem is not the queryset itself. The problem is the link generation around that queryset.

In this recipe, we will use it so that list pages remain stable, filters stay in place during navigation, and our templates no longer need manual query-string stitching.

Preserving Query State

The most useful way to think about the querystring tag is that it starts with the current request query and then lets us replace or add only the parameters we care about. When a user is already on a filtered snippet list, moving to the next page should not clear the active language filter or selected tag.

Likewise, changing the sort order should not drop the current page size or search term. If the template has access to request, the tag can use **`request.GET`** by default and then apply updates to it. It keeps the template concise because we no longer need loops, conditional checks, or hand-built **`?key=value`** strings just to preserve state across links. It also reduces subtle mistakes with duplicated parameters or lost filter values.

```
<a href="{% querystring page=page_obj.next_page_number
%}">Next</a>
```

This above one line expresses the exact behavior we want. It also makes pagination feel stable from the user's perspective because the current browsing context moves forward with them instead of being dropped at every click.

Using Tag for Filter Controls and Resetting Page

A filtered page often needs a second behavior alongside pagination, like whenever a filter changes, the current page number should usually reset to the first page. If a user is on page 5 and then selects a different language or tag, staying on page 5 may produce confusing or empty results. The **querystring** tag makes that easy to express because we can preserve the current query, replace the filter parameter, and set **page=1** at the same time.

```
<a href="{% querystring language='PY' page=1 %}">Python</a>

<a href="{% querystring language='JS' page=1
%}">JavaScript</a>

<a href="{% querystring language=None page=1 %}">All
Languages</a>
```

This above pattern keeps the filter links stable and predictable. The first two links set a filter and reset pagination. The third clears the language filter and also returns the user to the first page. That None behavior is especially useful because it lets us remove one parameter without rebuilding the entire URL manually.

Combining Pagination, Sorting, and Filters

In a manually assembled URL, every link would need to know about every other active parameter, which quickly becomes brittle and repetitive. With the tag, each link can focus on the one value it needs to change. A sort link can preserve filters and pagination state or deliberately reset the page. A tag filter link can preserve the search term. A paginator link can preserve both filter and sort choices. The more moving parts a list page has, the more helpful this becomes.

```
<a href="{% querystring sort='recent' page=1 %}">Most
Recent</a>

<a href="{% querystring sort='title' page=1 %}">Title</a>

{% if page_obj.has_previous %}

    <a href="{% querystring page=page_obj.previous_page_number
%}">Previous</a>

{% endif %}

<span>Page {{ page_obj.number }} of {{
page_obj.paginator.num_pages }}</span>
```

```
{% if page_obj.has_next %}
    <a href="{% querystring page=page_obj.next_page_number
%}">Next</a>
{% endif %}
```

What looked like a small template convenience turns out to be a powerful way to keep browsing state coherent without cluttering the template with procedural logic. That is exactly the kind of refinement that makes a Django application feel smoother and more dependable in daily use.

In this recipe, the real gain is not only fewer lines of template code. The real gain is consistency. The links now preserve context by default, which means users do not have to rebuild their filter state every time they navigate. It makes list pages feel much more polished, and it keeps the template layer focused on declarative navigation rather than manual query-string assembly.

Recipe 7: Optimizing Template Loading

The thing is, rendering templates is a basic part of serving content in Django, and as the number of templates goes up, the cost of finding, putting together, and rendering them can become more noticeable. It's not usually the first thing to hold things up in a small app, but it becomes more important as the project gets more screens, more shared fragments and more dynamic content. If your template layer is slow or overly complex, it can increase response time and make the application feel heavier than it needs to. The way we organise inheritance, reusable fragments, loaders, and rendering paths affects how quickly Django can produce the final response.

So, the reason of this recipe is to keep template loading efficient by choosing sensible loaders, keeping reuse patterns disciplined, and reducing unnecessary rendering overhead without making the template system harder to understand.

Using Cached Template Loaders in Production

The Django can cache compiled templates through the cached loader, which means repeated requests for the same templates do not pay the full compilation cost every time. The practical advantage is that our application still uses the same templates and the same inheritance structure, but repeated rendering becomes cheaper because Django can skip repeated compilation work.

```
TEMPLATES = [
    {
        "BACKEND":
"django.template.backends.django.DjangoTemplates",
        "DIRS": [BASE_DIR / "templates"],
```

```
        "APP_DIRS": False,
        "OPTIONS": {
            "loaders": [
                (
                    "django.template.loaders.cached.Loader",
                    [

"django.template.loaders.filesystem.Loader",

"django.template.loaders.app_directories.Loader",
                    ],
                ),
            ],
            "context_processors": [
                "django.template.context_processors.request",
                "django.template.context_processors.static",
                "django.template.context_processors.media",
                "django.template.context_processors.csrf",

"django.contrib.messages.context_processors.messages",
            ],
        },
    },
]
```

The configuration remains straightforward, which makes it a good fit for a chapter that aims to improve performance without forcing the template layer into something unfamiliar or brittle. It gives Django one cached entry point for template loading while still letting templates be discovered in both project-level and app-level locations. That means we gain performance without changing the way the template tree is organized.

Keeping Inheritance and Fragment Reuse

What affects how quickly templates load is not only how we set up the loaders, but also how we structure the templates themselves. It's easy to get things wrong when you're working on a template, like having too many includes or making it hard to read the code. A healthy structure uses inheritance for page-level layout, partials or includes for repeated fragments, and avoids pushing either pattern beyond what the template actually needs. If a two-level structure is enough, a page shouldn't inherit through several levels of layout wrappers. Also, not every three-line snippet that's been used a few times has to become something that can be reused. As a general rule, the more intentional and restrained your template tree is, the better your performance and readability will be. The idea is to use reuse where it gets rid of real duplication without making the structure too complicated.

Summary

Overall, we explored Django's template system and how it helped to build a presentation layer. We worked through advanced template inheritance so that shared layout elements such as headers, navigation, footers, and page sections could live in a stable base template while child templates supplied the content specific to each screen. We also used custom filters to keep presentation-focused transformations close to the template layer, which made our pages easier to read and helped us avoid repeating small formatting logic in multiple places. After that, we introduced reusable template partials.

Later, we then learned to manage static assets and user-uploaded media in a cleaner way by separating their purposes and configuring storage through Django's STORAGES setting. We also explored custom template tags for dynamic content, fragment caching for performance, and the querystring tag for preserving filters and pagination state across navigation. Finally, we examined template loading performance and saw disciplined inheritance, careful fragment reuse, and cached template loaders for efficient rendering.

CHAPTER 5: MASTERING FORMS AND USER INTERACTION

Overview

This chapter will focus on, how users will submit information and how the application will respond to that input in a clear, efficient, and safe way. In this chapter, we will start with learning formsets and inline formsets to manage multiple related forms in a single interface for group editing or repeated input. We will work with custom form fields and widgets so we can shape both the way data is entered and the way it is processed. We will then move into modern widgets and BoundField customization, where we will improve rendering consistency, error presentation, and the overall usability of the form layer without making the templates unnecessarily repetitive.

As the chapter progresses, we will explore how forms will become more interactive through asynchronous requests that provide quick feedback without replacing Django's normal validation flow. We will also apply advanced validation techniques so that field-specific rules, cross-field checks, and reusable validation logic will work together cleanly. After that, we will handle file uploads through forms using a storage-aware setup, examine multi-step forms for longer submission workflows, and finish by strengthening form security against common web attacks. By the end, we gain a definitive approach to design forms that will feel responsive to users, remain manageable in code, and protect both, application and its data with utmost effectiveness.

Recipe 1: Using Formsets and Inline Formsets

When a page needs to collect or edit several related records at once, handling one form at a time quickly becomes awkward for us and the users. In our app, we may want to create several snippets in one submission, edit multiple snippet records in one screen, or manage a parent object together with its children without forcing the user through a separate form for each related row. This is where formsets and inline formsets are useful. A formset gives us a structured way to work with multiple forms of the same type on one page, while an inline formset lets us manage related child objects alongside a parent model.

Our real learning in this recipe is going to be, to keep the grouped editing experience clean and predictable, while using the right formset type for the kind of save behavior we expect.

Using Model Formset

A grouped editing screen that works with model records should use a model formset, not a plain formset built from a **ModelForm**. We can define the model form exactly as before, then build a model formset around it and save the group in one clear step. If the page is about several snippet records, the formset should understand snippets directly.

```
from django.forms import ModelForm, modelformset_factory
from .models import Snippet
class SnippetForm(ModelForm):
```

```
    class Meta:
        model = Snippet
        fields = ["title", "code", "language"]
SnippetFormSet = modelformset_factory(
    Snippet,
    form=SnippetForm,
    extra=3,
    can_delete=True,
)
```

In the view, we instantiate the formset much like any other form, but now we can save the grouped records directly because the formset knows it is working with model instances. We validate the formset, save it when valid, and then return the user to the relevant page or show a success message.

The management form still matters because Django uses it to keep track of how many forms are present and how they should be processed. The template should therefore render **{{ formset.management_form }}** before iterating through the individual forms.

```
from django.shortcuts import redirect, render
from .forms import SnippetFormSet
def add_snippets(request):
    if request.method == "POST":
        formset = SnippetFormSet(request.POST, 
queryset=Snippet.objects.none())
        if formset.is_valid():
            formset.save()
            return redirect("snippets:snippet_list")
    else:
        formset = 
SnippetFormSet(queryset=Snippet.objects.none())
    return render(request, "snippets/add_snippets.html", 
{"formset": formset})
<form method="post">
```

```
    {% csrf_token %}
    {{ formset.management_form }}
    {% for form in formset %}
        {{ form.as_p }}
    {% endfor %}
    <button type="submit">Submit</button>
</form>
```

Using Inline Formset

Inline formsets become the better choice when the page edits a parent object together with several related child objects. In our app, let us consider that we manage a **SnippetCollection** and all the snippets inside that collection are on one screen. In that case, the relation between parent and child is part of the form design itself, and the inline formset gives us a much more natural way to express that than a generic formset would. We define the parent and child relationship once, then let Django generate the editing structure that belongs to that relationship.

```
from django.forms import inlineformset_factory
from .models import SnippetCollection, Snippet
CollectionSnippetFormSet = inlineformset_factory(
    SnippetCollection,
    Snippet,
    fields=["title", "code", "language"],
    extra=2,
    can_delete=True,
)
from django.shortcuts import get_object_or_404, redirect,
render
from .forms import CollectionSnippetFormSet
from .models import SnippetCollection
def edit_collection(request, collection_id):
    collection = get_object_or_404(SnippetCollection,
pk=collection_id)
```

```
    if request.method == "POST":
        formset = CollectionSnippetFormSet(request.POST,
instance=collection)
        if formset.is_valid():
            formset.save()
            return redirect("snippets:collection_detail",
collection_id=collection.id)
    else:
        formset =
CollectionSnippetFormSet(instance=collection)
    return render(
        request,
        "snippets/edit_collection.html",
        {"collection": collection, "formset": formset},
    )
```

Here, in this recipe, the formset is still our tool for managing multiple forms on one page, and an inline formset is still the natural extension of that idea when the forms belong to a parent-child relationship. The main difference in practice is that we now use the right factory for the right job, which means our save path is cleaner, our templates stay familiar, and our grouped editing workflows behave exactly the way the interface promises.

Recipe 2: Writing Custom Form Fields and Widgets

A form becomes more useful when it matches the shape of the data we actually want to collect rather than forcing the user into awkward input patterns. A custom field can define how raw input becomes Python data and how validation should behave. A custom widget can shape the HTML and browser-facing attributes.

In this recipe, we will build a custom field and widget pair that does useful work, then connect that field to a rendering pattern that keeps errors and labels clear and consistent.

Creating Custom Field

A custom field should earn its place by doing work that a built-in field does not already do well.

A comma-separated collaborator field is a good example because the browser still presents one text input, but our Python code wants a cleaned list of addresses. The field can therefore normalize the text into a list and validate each item before the form ever reaches the save step. This is a useful pattern because it shows us where field logic belongs. The field is responsible for turning raw user input into a clean Python value and rejecting invalid input early.

```
from django import forms
from django.core.exceptions import ValidationError
from django.core.validators import validate_email
class CommaSeparatedEmailsField(forms.CharField):
    default_error_messages = {
        "invalid_email": "%(email)s is not a valid email 
address.",
    }
    def to_python(self, value):
        if not value:
            return []
        return [email.strip() for email in value.split(",") if 
email.strip()]
    def validate(self, value):
        super().validate(value)
        for email in value:
            try:
                validate_email(email)
            except ValidationError:
                raise ValidationError(
                    self.error_messages["invalid_email"],
                    code="invalid_email",
                    params={"email": email},
                )
```

This field now gives us a clean list of addresses in **cleaned_data** instead of a raw string that still needs parsing. That small change makes downstream logic much easier. We can iterate through collaborator addresses, compare them, or store them without repeating string-splitting code in the view. It also means validation errors stay attached to the field itself, which is exactly what we want from a form.

Pairing Field with Widget

A widget does not validate data, but it strongly shapes the user experience because it controls the rendered HTML and the browser-facing attributes. If the field expects comma-separated emails, the widget should help the user understand that expectation clearly. A placeholder, a helpful CSS class, and a more descriptive input purpose can make the field much easier to use without changing the underlying validation logic at all.

```
from django.forms.widgets import TextInput
class EmailInputWidget(TextInput):
    input_type = "text"
    template_name = "widgets/email_input.html"
    def __init__(self, attrs=None):
        default_attrs = {
            "class": "email-input",
            "placeholder": "Enter emails separated by commas",
            "spellcheck": "false",
            "autocomplete": "off",
        }
        if attrs:
            default_attrs.update(attrs)
        super().__init__(default_attrs)
from django import forms
class InviteCollaboratorsForm(forms.Form):
    collaborators = CommaSeparatedEmailsField(
        widget=EmailInputWidget(),
        help_text="Separate each email with a comma.",
    )
```

This above pairing gives us a field that cleans and validates correctly and a widget that presents the input in a more helpful way. The field and widget now cooperate rather than overlap. One shapes the meaning of the data, and the other shapes the way the user experiences the input element. It is the pattern we want to carry forward into more advanced forms.

Rendering Errors and Labels

The Django 6.0 gives us a stronger rendering path through each field's bound representation, including **as_field_group()**, **aria-describedby**, and customizable **BoundField** behavior. It allows us to centralize the shape of a field instead of rebuilding label and error markup by hand in every template. It also improves accessibility because the error list and help text can be associated with the input automatically through rendered attributes and field-aware error output.

```
{{ form.non_field_errors }}
<div class="field-row">
    {{ form.collaborators.as_field_group }}
</div>
```

If we need finer control, we can still render the bound field manually:

```
{{ form.non_field_errors }}
<div class="field-row{% if form.collaborators.errors %} has-
errors{% endif %}">
    {{ form.collaborators.label_tag }}
    {{ form.collaborators }}
    {% if form.collaborators.help_text %}
        <p class="helptext" id="{{
form.collaborators.id_for_label }}_help">
            {{ form.collaborators.help_text }}
        </p>
    {% endif %}
    {{ form.collaborators.errors }}
</div>
```

This pattern gives us a reliable way to present validation feedback without scattering error markup logic across the entire project. A good error rendering pattern is therefore not only about style. It is also about preserving a reliable connection between the field, its help text, and its validation state.

The field already knows its label, its generated id, its errors, and its help text, so the template can stay focused on layout rather than reconstructing field state from scratch. It is the real gain from **BoundField**-aware rendering. We keep the form templates cleaner, and we make error presentation easier to standardize.

Recipe 3: Using Modern Widgets and BoundField Customization

Many forms do not need a fully custom field class, but they still benefit from better defaults, clearer browser semantics, and more consistent rendering behavior. A profile theme color is better represented with a color picker than with a plain text box. A search box should announce itself as a search field. A contact number should render like a telephone input instead of an ordinary text input.

In this recipe, we will combine the above discussed two improvements. We will use modern built-in widgets where they fit naturally, and we will customize BoundField behavior so our forms render with a cleaner and more predictable structure.

Using Built-in Modern Widgets

A form becomes easier to use when widget matches the user's intent. The Django's ColorInput, SearchInput, and TelInput are valuable precisely because they make that match clearer. They render HTML elements whose input types communicate purpose to the browser and to assistive tools, and in some cases they can unlock browser features such as built-in affordances or optimized input modes. That means we should reach for them when the data really is a color, a search query, or a telephone number rather than defaulting to a plain text widget for everything.

```
from django import forms
class ProfilePreferencesForm(forms.Form):
    display_name = forms.CharField(max_length=100)
    accent_color = forms.CharField(
        widget=forms.ColorInput(),
        help_text="Choose the color used in our public profile
card.",
    )
    snippet_search = forms.CharField(
```

```
        required=False,
        widget=forms.SearchInput(attrs={"placeholder": "Search
snippets"}),
    )
    contact_number = forms.CharField(
        required=False,
        widget=forms.TelInput(attrs={"placeholder": "Enter our
phone number"}),
    )
```

These above widgets are simple to adopt, and that is exactly why they are useful. We do not have to build a custom widget just to render an input with the correct browser-facing type. We can keep the form definition compact while still giving the rendered HTML a more meaningful shape.

Customizing Boundfield Behavior

A form-level **`bound_field_class`** enables us to add behavior that every rendered field on that form can share, such as extra wrapper classes or label styling. Instead of repeating the same extra CSS classes or field-state checks manually, we can let the bound field shape that behavior once and reuse it for all fields in the form.

```
from django import forms
class StyledBoundField(forms.BoundField):
    def css_classes(self, extra_classes=None):
        classes = super().css_classes(extra_classes)
        return f"form-field {classes}".strip()
    def label_tag(self, contents=None, attrs=None,
label_suffix=None, tag=None):
        attrs = attrs or {}
        existing = attrs.get("class", "")
        attrs["class"] = f"{existing} form-label".strip()
        return super().label_tag(contents, attrs,
label_suffix, tag)
class ProfilePreferencesForm(forms.Form):
    bound_field_class = StyledBoundField
```

```
    display_name = forms.CharField(max_length=100)
    accent_color = forms.CharField(widget=forms.ColorInput())
    snippet_search = forms.CharField(required=False,
widget=forms.SearchInput())
    contact_number = forms.CharField(required=False,
widget=forms.TelInput())
```

This change gives us a more consistent field presentation without requiring every template to rebuild the same visual rules. It also scales well. When the form grows, the rendering behavior stays stable because the fields inherit the same wrapper and label logic.

Using Improved Error and Accessibility Rendering

A modern field-rendering pattern should not stop at CSS classes. It should also preserve a clean relationship between the field, its help text, and its errors. The Bound fields can expose rendering helpers and accessibility-aware properties that make that easier to do consistently.

```
{{ form.non_field_errors }}
<div class="profile-preferences-form">
    {{ form.display_name.as_field_group }}
    {{ form.accent_color.as_field_group }}
    {{ form.snippet_search.as_field_group }}
    {{ form.contact_number.as_field_group }}
</div>
```

When we render a field group through the bound field, the field can carry its own label, widget, help text, and error output in a coordinated way. That means our templates can stay focused on layout while the field keeps its rendering state coherent.

Overall, this recipe shows us a clean middle path between custom field engineering and plain default rendering. It gives us a form layer that is more expressive, more maintainable, and better aligned with real user interaction without requiring us to reinvent every field from scratch.

Recipe 4: Implementing AJAX for Dynamic UI

It's more helpful if a form responds while you're typing rather than waiting for the whole page to reload after you submit your details. There are a few places in GitforGits that are great for this kind of thing. We might want to check if a snippet title is already being used by the current author, show a live validation message, or update a preview panel without interrupting the rest of the form. The key thing is that the enhancement should improve the form without making the server-side validation optional. So, a modern AJAX pattern needs two things. It should give you immediate feedback in the browser, and it should be a progressive enhancement rather than the only validation method.

In this recipe, we're aiming to create that pattern in a way that's easy to follow with fetch(), a special JSON endpoint, clear feedback elements, and safe CSRF handling for asynchronous requests.

Creating Lightweight JSON Validation Endpoint

The server-side part of the feature should stay narrow and focused. We are not submitting the entire form asynchronously here. We are validating one interaction point so the user can get early feedback before a normal form submission occurs. A good example is checking whether the current user already has a snippet with the same title. The endpoint should accept JSON, inspect the relevant value, and return a concise JSON response that says whether the proposed title is available and, if not, what message should be shown.

```
import json
from django.contrib.auth.decorators import login_required
from django.http import JsonResponse
from django.views.decorators.http import require_POST
from .models import Snippet
@login_required
@require_POST
def validate_snippet_title(request):
    payload = json.loads(request.body or "{}")
    title = (payload.get("title") or "").strip()
    if not title:
        return JsonResponse(
            {
                "is_valid": False,
                "message": "Please enter a title before 
checking availability.",
            }
```

```
        )
    exists = Snippet.objects.filter(author=request.user,
title__iexact=title).exists()
    if exists:
        return JsonResponse(
            {
                "is_valid": False,
                "message": "You already have a snippet with
this title.",
            }
        )
    return JsonResponse(
        {
            "is_valid": True,
            "message": "This title is available.",
        }
    )
```

This endpoint keeps its contract very small. It receives one value, applies one rule, and returns one concise result. This makes it easier to reuse and easier to test. It also keeps the feature from growing into a second full form-processing flow that duplicates the logic of the main submission endpoint. This makes the interaction predictable and keeps the validation rule grounded on the server, where it still belongs. The browser gets faster feedback, but the server remains the final authority.

Our normal form submission still performs the final validation and save. The AJAX endpoint simply gives the user earlier insight into one likely validation outcome. That division is what makes the pattern safe and maintainable instead of turning it into a fragile duplicate implementation of the entire form.

Exposing Endpoint through Route and Form Template

Now we give the endpoint a URL and wire the form template so the browser can interact with it. The template should include a normal CSRF token in the form, the input element we want to enhance, and a small feedback region that can display status text as the user types. A live region works well here because it lets validation messages be announced as they change. The form itself should still submit normally. The safest mental model is that AJAX assists the form, but the form still owns the actual submission path.

```
from django.urls import path
from .views import validate_snippet_title
urlpatterns = [
    path(
        "ajax/validate-snippet-title/",
        validate_snippet_title,
        name="validate_snippet_title",
    ),
]
<form method="post" id="snippet-form">
    {% csrf_token %}
    {{ form.non_field_errors }}
    <div class="field-row">
        {{ form.title.label_tag }}
        {{ form.title }}
        {{ form.title.errors }}
        <p id="title-feedback" aria-live="polite"></p>
    </div>
    <div class="field-row">
        {{ form.code.as_field_group }}
    </div>
    <div class="field-row">
        {{ form.language.as_field_group }}
    </div>
    <button type="submit">Save snippet</button>
</form>
```

This above template keeps the form fully functional even before the JavaScript enhancement runs. The live feedback element is simply waiting to be updated if JavaScript is available. It makes the form more resilient and avoids coupling the entire feature to one script block. It also keeps our design honest.

Using Fetch with Debouncing, Cancellation, and CSRF-safe Headers

The client-side code should be responsive without becoming noisy. A small debounce helps us wait until the user pauses typing, and an **AbortController** helps us cancel stale requests when new input arrives before the earlier request completes. For CSRF protection, a POST request should send the token in the **X-CSRFToken** header. The cleanest place to retrieve it is the hidden CSRF token input already present in the form. It keeps the script aligned with the existing form rather than depending on hard-coded values or brittle template injection patterns.

```
<script>
const titleInput = document.getElementById("id_title");
const feedback = document.getElementById("title-feedback");
const csrfToken =
document.querySelector("[name=csrfmiddlewaretoken]").value;
let timeoutId = null;
let controller = null;
titleInput.addEventListener("input", () => {
    const title = titleInput.value.trim();
    clearTimeout(timeoutId);
    if (controller) {
        controller.abort();
    }
    if (!title) {
        feedback.textContent = "";
        return;
    }
    timeoutId = setTimeout(async () => {
        controller = new AbortController();
        try {
```

```
            const response = await fetch(
                "{% url 'snippets:validate_snippet_title' %}",
                {
                    method: "POST",
                    headers: {
                        "Content-Type": "application/json",
                        "X-CSRFToken": csrfToken,
                    },
                    body: JSON.stringify({ title }),
                    signal: controller.signal,
                }
            );
            const data = await response.json();
            feedback.textContent = data.message;
            feedback.className = data.is_valid ? "valid-
message" : "error-message";
        } catch (error) {
            if (error.name !== "AbortError") {
                feedback.textContent = "Could not validate the
title right now.";
                feedback.className = "error-message";
            }
        }
    }, 300);
});
</script>
```

This above script does not try to take over the form. It simply adds a live validation layer around one field. The debounce keeps requests under control, the abort logic prevents stale responses from winning the race, and the feedback element updates in place without forcing a page reload. Most importantly, the code remains easy to reason about because it has one responsibility. It validates the title asynchronously. The form still performs its usual submit cycle, and the server still performs its usual final validation when the user actually saves the snippet.

The above demonstration is the right balance for interactive forms. Using it, we can improve the user experience without weakening the form's real safety checks or making the codebase harder to maintain.

Recipe 5: Applying Advanced Form Validation

Most forms don't just stop at checking if a field is empty or if a value is the right type. Our app shows us a few examples where validation needs to express business rules as well as syntax rules. For example, a snippet might need to reject dangerous keywords, two fields might need to be checked together, and a rule might need to remain true whether the data came from a browser form, a shell session, or an import job. The Django's validation flow is great for this because it lets us validate at the field level, at the form level, and, when needed, at the model level as well.

In this recipe, we're aiming to make sure everyone knows what they're responsible for. A field-level rule should stay close to the field that owns it, a cross-field rule should live in **clean()**, and reusable validation logic should be extracted into validators that can be shared across forms or models.

Validating Individual Fields and Forms

A strong validation design begins by giving each rule the narrowest home that fits it. If a rule concerns one field only, we place it in **clean_<fieldname>()** or in a validator. If a rule depends on the relationship between fields, we move it into the form's clean() method. It maintains the form readable because we do not force one large validation method to do every job at once.

```
from django import forms
from django.core.exceptions import ValidationError
from .models import Snippet
def validate_not_empty(value):
    if not value.strip():
        raise ValidationError("This field cannot be empty.")
class SnippetForm(forms.ModelForm):
    title = forms.CharField(validators=[validate_not_empty])
    class Meta:
        model = Snippet
```

```
        fields = ["title", "code", "language"]
    def clean_code(self):
        code = self.cleaned_data["code"]
        banned_keywords = ["exec", "eval"]
        for keyword in banned_keywords:
            if keyword in code:
                raise ValidationError(f"Usage of '{keyword}' 
is not allowed.")
        return code
    def clean(self):
        cleaned_data = super().clean()
        title = cleaned_data.get("title")
        code = cleaned_data.get("code")
        if title and code and title.lower() in code.lower():
            self.add_error(
                "code",
                "The code snippet should not contain the 
title.",
            )
        return cleaned_data
```

In the snippet form above, the code field blocks unsafe keywords, while the form-level **`clean()`** method checks whether the title is being repeated inside the snippet body in a way that hurts the quality of the submission. The form therefore communicates two very different ideas cleanly. One rule protects the content of a single field, and the other protects the relationship between two fields.

Keeping Model-Level Rules Authoritative

A form is an important validation layer, but it is not the only way data enters the application. If a rule should remain true no matter how an object is created or updated, then the model should also participate. This is why Django's model validation still matters even in a chapter focused on forms. A **`ModelForm`** will call into model validation for the included model fields, which helps us keep data logic close to the data itself instead of scattering it across many forms.

```
from django.core.exceptions import ValidationError
from django.db import models
class Snippet(models.Model):
    title = models.CharField(max_length=100)
    code = models.TextField()
    language = models.CharField(max_length=50)
    def clean(self):
        if self.title and self.code and self.title.lower() in
self.code.lower():
            raise ValidationError(
                {"code": "The code snippet should not contain
the title."}
            )
```

This is especially useful for rules that define the validity of the object rather than the convenience of one user interface. In practice, this means we can let the form own user-facing checks and field presentation, while the model continues to guard the object's deeper integrity. That balance keeps our validation system robust without making any single layer carry too much responsibility.

Recipe 6: Handling File Uploads with Forms

If you need to attach supporting documents or add richer content to a snippet submission, you can do that too. The problem is that a file upload isn't just another field on a form. It brings storage, validation, security, and user feedback into the same workflow. A file needs to be received from **`request.FILES`**, validated for size and type, stored through the configured storage backend, and then exposed back to the template in a safe and predictable way. The Django's file handling is still nice and straightforward, but it's better to use the **`STORAGE`** model for uploads instead of the older ways.

This recipe's aim is to keep the upload form simple, make sure the uploaded file is valid, and let the project's configured default storage decide where the content should be stored.

Storing and Validating Uploaded files

A file upload form begins with the model and the form, but the real flow only becomes correct when we remember the storage layer as well. The model field such as **`FileField`** will use the project's default storage backend, which is configured in **`STORAGES["default"]`**. That means our form code does not need to hard-code local paths or file handling logic. It only needs to validate the file and save the model instance. A simple validator that checks size and allowed extensions is a good starting point because it protects both resources and user expectations.

```
from django import forms
from django.core.exceptions import ValidationError
from .models import Snippet
class SnippetForm(forms.ModelForm):
    class Meta:
        model = Snippet
        fields = ["title", "code", "language", "file"]
    def clean_file(self):
        file = self.cleaned_data["file"]
        if file.size > 5 * 1024 * 1024:
            raise ValidationError("File size must be under 5 MB.")
        allowed_extensions = (".py", ".txt", ".md")
        if not file.name.lower().endswith(allowed_extensions):
            raise ValidationError("Only .py, .txt, and .md files are allowed.")
        return file
<form method="post" enctype="multipart/form-data">
    {% csrf_token %}
    {{ form.as_p }}
    <button type="submit">Upload</button>
</form>
```

The form still needs **enctype="multipart/form-data"** in the HTML, and the view still needs **request.FILES**, because uploaded files arrive separately from ordinary **POST** data. When we keep those pieces aligned, the upload path becomes straightforward and easy to reason about.

Configuring STORAGES for Static Assets Separation

The static files belong to our codebase and deployment process. And, the uploaded files belong to the running application and to the users who create them. The Django's **STORAGES** setting makes that distinction explicit by giving the default uploaded-file storage and the staticfiles storage separate roles.

For an ordinary local setup, the default storage can use **FileSystemStorage**, while static files continue to use the staticfiles backend. Once that is in place, our form view only needs to save the form.

```
# settings.py
STORAGES = {
    "default": {
        "BACKEND":
"django.core.files.storage.FileSystemStorage",
    },
    "staticfiles": {
        "BACKEND":
"django.contrib.staticfiles.storage.StaticFilesStorage",
    },
}
MEDIA_URL = "/media/"
MEDIA_ROOT = BASE_DIR / "media"
from django.shortcuts import redirect, render
from .forms import SnippetForm
def upload_snippet(request):
    if request.method == "POST":
        form = SnippetForm(request.POST, request.FILES)
        if form.is_valid():
            form.save()
            return redirect("snippets:snippet_list")
    else:
        form = SnippetForm()
```

```
    return render(request, "snippets/upload_form.html",
{"form": form})
```

The file field uses the default storage backend automatically, and later deployment choices can change that backend without forcing a rewrite of the form-handling code itself. That separation is the real value of the **STORAGES** approach. It keeps the storage policy in settings and keeps the form code focused on validation and saving.

The form still does what the reader expects. It accepts the uploaded file, validates it, and saves the object. The difference is that the storage responsibility is now expressed clearly in settings rather than being left implicit. This makes our upload story stronger, because a form that handles files well is never only about **request.FILES**.

Recipe 7: Building Multi-step Forms

One thing I've noticed is that long forms can get tiring when they ask you to enter lots of related information on one screen. It's often better to break that process down into smaller steps, because then it's easier to understand and you're more likely to get everything done. In our app, we've got some great examples of this pattern, like submitting a detailed review workflow, creating a multi-part collaboration request, or gathering structured metadata before a final confirmation step. However, a multi-step form needs more than just multiple templates. It's got to keep track of the state between steps, make sure each stage is validated correctly, and then put all the data together into one final save path at the end.

The idea with this recipe is to keep the original session-based approach because it still teaches the right lesson clearly. We'll go through each step, store any intermediate cleaned data in the session, and then consolidate it safely when the user reaches the final submission stage.

Storing and Restoring Cleaned Step Data

A session-backed flow works well for a multi-step form because it enable us keep temporary progress without saving incomplete data to the database too early. The key to making this manageable is namespacing our session keys clearly and always storing cleaned form data rather than raw **POST** data.

```
def step_one(request):docs
    initial_data = request.session.get("code_review_step1",
{})
    form = StepOneForm(initial=initial_data)
    if request.method == "POST":
        form = StepOneForm(request.POST)
```

```
        if form.is_valid():
            request.session["code_review_step1"] =
form.cleaned_data
            return redirect("reviews:step_two")
    return render(request, "reviews/step_one.html", {"form":
form})
def step_two(request):
    initial_data = request.session.get("code_review_step2",
{})
    form = StepTwoForm(initial=initial_data)
    if request.method == "POST":
        form = StepTwoForm(request.POST)
        if form.is_valid():
            request.session["code_review_step2"] =
form.cleaned_data
            return redirect("reviews:confirm_review")
    return render(request, "reviews/step_two.html", {"form":
form})
```

here, the cleaned data gives us a more dependable state snapshot, because each step has already passed validation before its values are written into the session. We can then reuse those values as initial data if the user returns to an earlier step, which keeps the process smoother and reduces the frustration of re-entering data.

Consolidating and Cleaning Session Data

The final step should gather the validated data from each earlier stage, create the relevant object or objects, and then clear the session entries that belonged to the in-progress workflow. A small amount of care here makes the overall process much more reliable. We should use **`pop()`** rather than **`del`** where practical so the cleanup remains safe even if a particular key is missing, and we should think of the final submission as the point where temporary workflow state becomes real persisted application data.

```
def confirm_review(request):
    if request.method == "POST":
        all_data = {
```

```
            **request.session.get("code_review_step1", {}),
            **request.session.get("code_review_step2", {}),
        }
        new_review = CodeReview.objects.create(**all_data)
        request.session.pop("code_review_step1", None)
        request.session.pop("code_review_step2", None)
        return redirect("reviews:success",
review_id=new_review.id)
    return render(request, "reviews/confirm_review.html")
```

The above perspective keeps the multi-step flow easy to reason about. Until the final step succeeds, the session contains temporary progress. Once it succeeds, the application owns the new object and the temporary state can disappear.

The session-based pattern is still a clear way to teach multi-step forms, and the refinements are mainly about keeping the keys organized and the cleanup safer. It makes the workflow easier to maintain without changing its overall shape.

Recipe 8: Securing Forms against Attacks

Forms are the part of any website that's most exposed because they're where user input meets the server-side behaviour. If we don't keep a close eye on them, they're at risk of cross-site scripting, cross-site request forgery, unsafe query patterns, and client-side tampering that tries to bypass our normal submission flow. Our app is not an exception to this. A snippet submission form, profile update form, or upload form all accept untrusted input, so we have to design them assuming that the browser can be manipulated and the incoming data can be hostile.

The agenda of this recipe is to keep Django's current protections in place, strengthen them with a CSP-aware posture, and adopt a modern client-side mindset in which browser-side checks improve usability but never replace the server as the final authority.

Keeping Server Validation Authoritative

The Django already gives us several important protections if we use it properly. Template rendering escapes variables by default to reduce cross-site scripting risk when user-provided content is displayed. Form handling includes CSRF protection when we include **`{% csrf_token %}`** and keep the CSRF middleware enabled. The ORM uses parameterized queries to protect from SQL injection patterns.

All these protections are strongest when we let Django do its job instead of bypassing the framework in the name of convenience.

```
<form method="post">
    {% csrf_token %}
    {{ form.non_field_errors }}
    {{ form.as_p }}
    <button type="submit">Submit</button>
</form>
```

A browser can help the user, but it must never be trusted as the judge of whether data is safe or valid.

Adding CSP-Aware Guidance

A stronger security posture in Django 6 includes Content Security Policy. The CSP helps the browser decide which sources of scripts, styles, and other content are trusted, which makes it much harder for injected content to execute. For forms, this matters because validation scripts, live previews, and interactive enhancements often tempt us to scatter inline JavaScript directly into templates. A safer approach is to prefer static JavaScript files for form behavior wherever possible.

```
# settings.py
from django.utils.csp import CSP
MIDDLEWARE = [
    "django.middleware.security.SecurityMiddleware",
    "django.contrib.sessions.middleware.SessionMiddleware",
    "django.middleware.common.CommonMiddleware",
    "django.middleware.csrf.CsrfViewMiddleware",
    "django.contrib.auth.middleware.AuthenticationMiddleware",

"django.middleware.content.ContentSecurityPolicyMiddleware",
]
SECURE_CSP = {
    "default-src": [CSP.SELF],
    "script-src": [CSP.SELF, CSP.NONCE],
```

```
    "style-src": [CSP.SELF],
}
<script nonce="{{ csp_nonce }}">
    // Use only when inline script is truly necessary.
</script>
```

When we truly need an inline script, we should let the page use a nonce-aware policy and supply the request-specific nonce through the template context rather than leaving the page open to broad inline execution. That means our forms layer should not only think about escaped output and CSRF. It should also think about how scripts are introduced into the page. A form with careful validation but a permissive script policy is still weaker than it needs to be.

Adopting Client-Side Hardening Posture

Client-side hardening still has value, but its role should stay clear. The browser-side validation, input types, autocomplete choices, and safer form markup improve the user experience and reduce accidental mistakes, yet they do not replace server-side checks. A modern posture means we use HTML features and JavaScript for guidance, not for trust. We can use **type="email"**, **type="tel"**, **maxlength**, and clear feedback regions to guide the user. We can avoid inline event handlers, keep JavaScript in static files where practical, and make sure asynchronous form helpers still send CSRF tokens correctly. We can also keep data upload limits and file-count limits in mind when designing upload-heavy forms, because request-level protections such as **DATA_UPLOAD_MAX_MEMORY_SIZE** and **DATA_UPLOAD_MAX_NUMBER_FILES** exist for a reason.

This recipe still protects against XSS, CSRF, and unsafe query usage, but we now place those protections inside a broader posture that also accounts for CSP, safer script delivery, and the idea that client-side checks should assist the user rather than define what the server will accept. That mindset is what keeps forms dependable as they become more interactive and more central to the application.

Summary

In this chapter, we explored how Django forms supported richer and more structured user interaction across our app. We began by working with formsets and inline formsets so that multiple related records could be created or edited together in one coherent interface. After that, we moved into custom form fields and widgets, where we shaped both the data-handling logic and the browser-facing input experience to suit the needs of the application more precisely. We also learned modern widgets and BoundField customization for improved rendering consistency, accessibility, and error presentation.

We then focused on responsiveness, validation, uploads, flow design, and security. Through asynchronous form interaction, we saw how dynamic feedback could be provided without disrupting the main submission flow, while still preserving server-side validation as the final authority. We strengthened validation further by applying field-level, form-level, and reusable validator patterns so the submitted data remained dependable and well structured. We also handled file uploads through forms using a cleaner storage-driven approach, then examined how multi-step forms could guide users through larger submission processes without overwhelming them. Finally, we secured the form layer against common attacks by relying on Django's built-in protections, improving client-side hardening, and adding a stronger CSP-aware posture so that user input could be processed in a safer and more trustworthy way.

CHAPTER 6: AUTHENTICATION AND AUTHORIZATION

Overview

This chapter takes us to how users identify themselves, how the application will decide what they are allowed to do, and how account security will remain dependable while the app develops. We will begin by shaping a custom user model so that the application can reflect our own account requirements rather than relying on a one-size-fits-all default. From there, we will build richer authentication flows that will include email verification, passwordless access patterns, and more deliberate link-based account checks. We will also introduce task-backed email delivery so that authentication messages such as verification and reset emails can be treated as structured background work instead of slowing down the request-response cycle.

Later, we will move into authorization wherein we will work with role-based permissions, groups, and social authentication patterns. We will strengthen the day-to-day account experience through safer session and cookie handling, more modern authentication form customization, and a practical approach to two-factor authentication. And lastly, we will rebuild the account activation and password reset flow. By the end of the chapter, we will have a complete and much stronger understanding of how Django will help us design authentication and authorization systems that are secure, flexible, and user-friendly.

Recipe 1: Setting up Custom User Models

At some point, almost every application needs a user model that reflects its own identity rather than settling for a generic default shape. A custom user model gives us that flexibility from the start. The main value of this recipe is that, it gives us a stable foundation for everything else that depends on user identity, including email verification, passwordless login, social authentication, and any account-specific workflow we introduce later. And, this is why the user model is worth shaping carefully before the rest of the authentication chapter builds on it.

Creating Custom User Model and Manager

We will begin with defining a custom manager, use email as the identifying field, keep **`is_active`** and **`is_staff`**, and inherit from **`AbstractBaseUser`** together with **`PermissionsMixin`**.

```
from django.db import models
from django.contrib.auth.models import (
    AbstractBaseUser,
    BaseUserManager,
    PermissionsMixin,
)
```

```
class CustomUserManager(BaseUserManager):
    def create_user(self, email, password=None,
**extra_fields):
        if not email:
            raise ValueError("The Email field must be set")
        email = self.normalize_email(email)
        user = self.model(email=email, **extra_fields)
        user.set_password(password)
        user.save(using=self._db)
        return user
    def create_superuser(self, email, password=None,
**extra_fields):
        extra_fields.setdefault("is_staff", True)
        extra_fields.setdefault("is_superuser", True)
        extra_fields.setdefault("is_active", True)
        if extra_fields.get("is_staff") is not True:
            raise ValueError("Superuser must have
is_staff=True.")
        if extra_fields.get("is_superuser") is not True:
            raise ValueError("Superuser must have
is_superuser=True.")
        return self.create_user(email, password,
**extra_fields)
class CustomUser(AbstractBaseUser, PermissionsMixin):
    email = models.EmailField(unique=True)
    is_active = models.BooleanField(default=True)
    is_staff = models.BooleanField(default=False)
    objects = CustomUserManager()
    USERNAME_FIELD = "email"
    REQUIRED_FIELDS = []
    def __str__(self):
```

```
        return self.email
```

It gives full control over the model while still retaining Django's password hashing and permission machinery. The only light tightening worth making is to ensure that **`create_superuser()`** explicitly guarantees the flags required for an actual superuser account.

Registering Model in Settings and Admin

The rest of the workflow remains straightforward. We point **`AUTH_USER_MODEL`** at the custom user class, run migrations, and then register the model with a suitable admin configuration so the user records remain manageable through Django's admin site.

```
AUTH_USER_MODEL = "accounts.CustomUser"
from django.contrib import admin
from django.contrib.auth.admin import UserAdmin
from .models import CustomUser
@admin.register(CustomUser)
lass CustomUserAdmin(UserAdmin):
    model = CustomUser
     st_display = ["email", "is_staff", "is_active"]
        ring = ["email"]
          ts = (
                {"fields": ("email", "password")}),
                sions", {"fields": ("is_active", "is_staff",
                 roups", "user_permissions")}),
                    dates", {"fields": ("last_login",)}),



                             e",),
                            mail", "password1", "password2",
```

```
            },
        ),
    )
python manage.py makemigrations
python manage.py migrate
```

In the above, the core pattern gives us the right foundation for the authentication flows that follow.

Recipe 2: Implementing Advanced User Authentication Flows

We often need to verify ownership of the email address, delay access until that verification is complete, support sign-in by email link instead of by remembered password, and keep the whole process responsive without forcing slow email delivery to happen directly inside the request-response cycle. An authentication system should not only let people sign in. It should also make account ownership clear, reduce friction where appropriate, and keep the security-sensitive steps deliberate and auditable.

The important learning in this recipe is that, the email-driven authentication actions should be treated as part of a structured workflow rather than as scattered helper functions that send messages inline and hope for the best. In Django 6.0's, the built-in Tasks framework exists precisely to move work such as email delivery out of the request-response cycle, while Django's email layer continues to support both simple wrappers and the more flexible EmailMessage/EmailMultiAlternatives API for richer messages.

Shaping Authentication Flow around States

A strong authentication flow usually becomes easier to reason about when we think in terms of account states. A user may be newly registered but not yet verified. A verified user may request a passwordless sign-in link. A sign-in link may be valid, expired, or already used. When we model the flow this way, the code stops feeling like a collection of unrelated views and starts behaving like one coherent system.

```
from django.db import models
from django.contrib.auth.models import (
    AbstractBaseUser,
    BaseUserManager,
```

```
    PermissionsMixin,
)
class CustomUserManager(BaseUserManager):
    def create_user(self, email, password=None,
**extra_fields):
        if not email:
            raise ValueError("The Email field must be set")
        email = self.normalize_email(email)
        user = self.model(email=email, **extra_fields)
        user.set_password(password)
        user.save(using=self._db)
        return user
class CustomUser(AbstractBaseUser, PermissionsMixin):
    email = models.EmailField(unique=True)
    email_verified = models.BooleanField(default=False)
    is_active = models.BooleanField(default=True)
    is_staff = models.BooleanField(default=False)
    objects = CustomUserManager()
    USERNAME_FIELD = "email"
    REQUIRED_FIELDS = []
```

In the above, we can keep the user model simple by adding an **email_verified** flag and treating verification as the gate that unlocks full account use. It keeps the core login identity centered on email while still enforcing that the email address has been proven to belong to the account holder.

This model keeps the account state focused and readable. We are not storing long-lived verification tokens or login tokens directly on the user record. Instead, we keep the durable account truth on the model and generate short-lived signed links when the workflow needs them.

Generating Signed Verification and Login Links

For email verification and passwordless login, the practical pattern is similar. We create a signed payload that identifies the user and the purpose of the link, then enforce an expiration time when the link is consumed. This lets the link remain short-lived and self-describing without forcing us to persist a random token field on the model each time the flow runs. It also means the verification and passwordless login views can share a similar style of implementation even though the outcome is different in each case. One flow confirms the email and redirects to login. The other logs the user in and redirects to the dashboard or snippet listing page.

```
from django.core import signing
VERIFICATION_SALT = "accounts.verify-email"
PASSWORDLESS_SALT = "accounts.passwordless-login"
def build_verification_token(user):
    return signing.dumps(
        {"user_id": user.pk, "purpose": "verify_email"},
        salt=VERIFICATION_SALT,
    )
def build_passwordless_token(user):
    return signing.dumps(
        {"user_id": user.pk, "purpose": "passwordless_login"},
        salt=PASSWORDLESS_SALT,
    )
from django.contrib.auth import get_user_model, login
from django.core import signing
from django.shortcuts import get_object_or_404, redirect
User = get_user_model()
def verify_email(request, token):
    payload = signing.loads(token, salt=VERIFICATION_SALT,
max_age=60 * 60 * 24)
    user = get_object_or_404(User, pk=payload["user_id"])
    user.email_verified = True
    user.save(update_fields=["email_verified"])
    return redirect("accounts:login")
def passwordless_login(request, token):
```

```
    payload = signing.loads(token, salt=PASSWORDLESS_SALT,
max_age=60 * 15)
    user = get_object_or_404(User, pk=payload["user_id"])
    if not user.email_verified:
        return redirect("accounts:login")
    login(request, user,
backend="django.contrib.auth.backends.ModelBackend")
    return redirect("dashboard")
```

Here in the above script, the key point is that, both flows remain server-driven and time-bounded. The email carries the link, but the server still decides whether the payload is authentic and still fresh before taking action. The verification links last longer because a new user may open the email hours later. And, the passwordless login links are shorter-lived because they are a direct sign-in credential and should expire quickly.

Using Modern Email API through Message-Building Helpers

When it comes to email delivery, it's best to think of the application as treating the email as a top-priority item rather than just a basic text string. I think a helper that builds an **EmailMultiAlternatives** object would be perfect, because it'll let us provide both plain text and HTML versions, set the sender cleanly, and keep the message definition in one place. This also fits well with the general direction of Django's email API, which keeps supporting **send_mail()** but is pushing people to use **EmailMessage**-style classes more. It's also worth keeping in mind how calls are made.

Since Django 6.0, most optional arguments have been replaced by keywords, which is another reason why the object-oriented email path often feels cleaner for non-trivial flows.

```
from django.conf import settings
from django.core.mail import EmailMultiAlternatives
from django.template.loader import render_to_string
from django.urls import reverse
def build_verification_email(user, token):
    verification_path = reverse("accounts:verify_email",
args=[token])
    verification_url =
f"{settings.SITE_URL}{verification_path}"
    context = {
```

```
        "user": user,
        "verification_url": verification_url,
    }
    subject = "Verify our GitforGits account"
    text_body =
render_to_string("accounts/emails/verify_email.txt", context)
    html_body =
render_to_string("accounts/emails/verify_email.html", context)
    message = EmailMultiAlternatives(
        subject=subject,
        body=text_body,
        from_email=settings.DEFAULT_FROM_EMAIL,
        to=[user.email],
    )
    message.attach_alternative(html_body, "text/html")
    return message
```

The same pattern can be used for a passwordless login email. Once these helper functions exist, the views no longer need to know how the email is built. They only need to know that a verification email or a login-link email should be requested. That is exactly the point where the Tasks framework becomes a natural next step, because email creation can remain structured while email delivery moves safely out of the request-response cycle.

Keeping Views focused on Workflow Transitions

A registration view should create the user, generate the verification token, and request that the email be sent. A passwordless request view should validate the submitted email, generate the sign-in token, and request that the login email be sent. The actual email dispatch should not slow down the response path. The view's responsibility is therefore to advance the workflow state, not to perform every supporting task inline.

```
from django.contrib import messages
from django.shortcuts import redirect, render
from .emails import build_verification_email
from .tokens import build_verification_token
```

```
from .tasks import send_email_message_task
def register(request):
    if request.method == "POST":
        form = RegistrationForm(request.POST)
        if form.is_valid():
            user = form.save()
            token = build_verification_token(user)
            message = build_verification_email(user, token)
            send_email_message_task.enqueue(
                subject=message.subject,
                body=message.body,
                from_email=message.from_email,
                to=message.to,
                alternatives=message.alternatives,
            )
            messages.success(request, "Check our email to
verify our account.")
            return redirect("accounts:login")
    else:
        form = RegistrationForm()
    return render(request, "accounts/register.html", {"form":
form})
```

The Django's Tasks framework handles task definition, validation, and queuing, but actual background execution requires a backend and a worker outside the request-response cycle, so production setups should be planned with that in mind.

In the above, the account state is explicit, signed links are short-lived and purpose-bound, email construction is modernized, and delivery is prepared to move through tasks instead of running inline in the view. It gives the authentication flow a cleaner structure and a more realistic path for a production-ready application.

Recipe 3: Sending Authentication Emails with

Django Tasks

Email-driven authentication workflows become much easier to manage when email delivery is treated as background work rather than as something the view must finish before returning a response. Activities like registration, verification, passwordless login, and password reset emails all benefit from that design because none of those actions should keep the browser waiting for SMTP delivery to complete. The Django 6.0's Tasks framework gives us a built-in way to define and enqueue work outside the request-response cycle. It defines the task and handles queuing and result handling, but it does not run the work itself. That execution still depends on the configured backend and the infrastructure behind it.

Configuring Task Backend for Development and Testing

Before we define the task itself, we need to decide how tasks behave in the current environment. The Immediate backend is useful when we want task calls to execute immediately while we are still wiring the feature together locally. The Dummy backend is useful when we want to inspect enqueued tasks without actually executing them.

```
# settings.py
TASKS = {
    "default": {
        "BACKEND":
"django.tasks.backends.immediate.ImmediateBackend",
    }
}
```

For tests where we want to inspect what was queued instead of sending messages, we can switch to:

```
# settings.py
TASKS = {
    "default": {
        "BACKEND": "django.tasks.backends.dummy.DummyBackend",
    }
}
```

These two settings give us a clean development path. We can build the authentication flow and task calls now, and then later plug in a production-ready backend without having to redesign the views that already enqueue work.

Defining Authentication Sending Email Task

A task should stay focused and serializable. For authentication emails, that usually means the task should receive the exact pieces it needs to send the message and then use Django's email classes to send it. One good pattern is to pass the subject, plain text body, sender, recipients, and optional HTML alternatives as simple values.

```
from django.core.mail import EmailMultiAlternatives
from django.tasks import task
@task
def send_email_message_task(subject, body, from_email, to, alternatives=None):
    message = EmailMultiAlternatives(
        subject=subject,
        body=body,
        from_email=from_email,
        to=to,
    )
    if alternatives:
        for content, mimetype in alternatives:
            message.attach_alternative(content, mimetype)
    message.send()
```

This task is intentionally narrow. It is not a general notification system. It is simply the mechanism that delivers one already-prepared email.

Queueing Verification and Reset Emails from Auth Flow

Once the task exists, the view creates the token, builds the message, and enqueues the task. That means the user gets a fast response and the heavy lifting moves into the task layer. The same pattern works for verification emails, passwordless login emails, and password reset emails. In each case the view stays focused on the authentication state transition, while the task system owns the delivery step.

```
def request_passwordless_login(request):
    if request.method == "POST":
```

```
        form = PasswordlessLoginRequestForm(request.POST)
        if form.is_valid():
            user = form.cleaned_data["user"]
            token = build_passwordless_token(user)
            message = build_passwordless_email(user, token)
            send_email_message_task.enqueue(
                subject=message.subject,
                body=message.body,
                from_email=message.from_email,
                to=message.to,
                alternatives=message.alternatives,
            )
            messages.success(request, "Check our email for our
sign-in link.")
            return redirect("accounts:login")
    else:
        form = PasswordlessLoginRequestForm()
    return render(request,
"accounts/request_passwordless_login.html", {"form": form})
```

The above same structure can be applied to account verification and password reset messages. It means our authentication emails all follow the same pattern, which makes the code easier to extend and easier to audit later.

Once authentication emails move into tasks, the overall auth flow becomes easier to scale and easier to reason about. The HTTP request creates or validates state. The email helper builds the message. The task layer delivers it. It is a much healthier design than having account creation, token generation, email composition, and SMTP communication all happen in one view function.

Recipe 4: Executing Role-based Permissions and Groups

There'll be different user roles, like administrators, content creators, and regular users, and they'll need different levels of access and permissions as the application progresses. So, to keep the platform secure and intact, it's vital to manage these roles and the permissions that come with them. In this recipe, we'll use Django's built-in groups and permissions framework to manage user capabilities and access rights throughout the application.

Defining User Groups and Permissions

So here, we begin by identifying the roles needed within our application and the specific permissions each role requires. The permissions in Django are typically tied to models and can be automatically generated for add, change, delete, and view operations.

```
from django.db import models
class Snippet(models.Model):
 # Model fields
 class Meta:
 permissions = [
 ("approve_snippet", "Can approve snippets"),
 ("feature_snippet", "Can mark snippets as featured"),
 ]
```

For custom permissions or more granular control, we can define them directly in our models.

Creating Groups and Assigning Permissions

We can make use of Django's admin site or shell to create groups corresponding to our roles and assign the relevant permissions to each group.

```
from django.contrib.auth.models import Group, Permission
# Creating a group for content creators
content_creators_group, created =
Group.objects.get_or_create(name='Content Creators')
# Fetching model permissions
add_snippet_perm =
Permission.objects.get(codename='add_snippet')
change_snippet_perm =
Permission.objects.get(codename='change_snippet')
# Assigning permissions to the group
```

```
content_creators_group.permissions.add(add_snippet_perm,
change_snippet_perm)
```

In the above, we created a "Content Creators" group with permissions to add and change snippets.

Assigning Users to Groups

We can also assign users to the appropriate groups based on their roles.

```
from django.contrib.auth.models import User
# Assuming you have a user instance
user = User.objects.get(username='johndoe')
user.groups.add(content_creators_group)
```

This can be done programmatically or through the Django admin interface.

Checking Permissions in Views

Within our views, we can also leverage Django's permission-checking utilities to control access.

```
from django.contrib.auth.decorators import permission_required
from django.contrib.auth.mixins import PermissionRequiredMixin
from django.views.generic import View
# For function-based views
@permission_required('snippets.add_snippet',
raise_exception=True)
def add_snippet(request):
 # View logic
# For class-based views
class FeatureSnippetView(PermissionRequiredMixin, View):
 permission_required = 'snippets.feature_snippet'
 # View logic
```

We can use decorators for function-based views and mixins for class-based views.

Overall, we can build an authorization system that is secure, scalable, and compatible with our apps varied requirements.

Recipe 5: Implementing OAuth and Social Authentication

There are a few things we could do to improve the login process for our app, and we're thinking about using OAuth and social authentication as a way to do this. And, it's not just that using OAuth and social authentication makes signing in easier, rather it also will help us to boost registration rates by taking advantage of the trust and familiarity that users already have with these platforms.

So, we will implement in the following steps:

Choosing Library

The **django-allauth** is a popular package that provides comprehensive support for social authentication, handling the complexities of OAuth protocols and integrating with a wide range of providers.

Here, we can start by installing **django-allauth** in our virtual env:

```
pip install django-allauth
```

Configuring 'settings.py'

After this, we then add **django.contrib.sites**, **allauth**, **allauth.account**, and **allauth.socialaccount** to our **INSTALLED_APPS**.

```
INSTALLED_APPS = [
 # Other apps...
 'django.contrib.sites',
 'allauth',
 'allauth.account',
 'allauth.socialaccount',
 # Providers (e.g., Google, Facebook)
 'allauth.socialaccount.providers.google',
]
AUTHENTICATION_BACKENDS = [
 'django.contrib.auth.backends.ModelBackend',
```

```
 'allauth.account.auth_backends.AuthenticationBackend',
]
SITE_ID = 1
```

In the above, we have also configured the Django sites framework by setting **SITE_ID**, typically to 1, and added the allauth's authentication backends

Updating URLs

Next, we then include **allauth** URLs in our project's **urls.py** to make the authentication views available:

```
urlpatterns = [
 # Other URLs...
 path('accounts/', include('allauth.urls')),
]
```

Next, we then visit the admin panel to configure the social apps, primarily Google and Facebook with the right credentials. So here, while **django-allauth** provides default templates, if we could customize them to match our application's look and feel, it is going to be a seamless user experience.

Recipe 6: Managing User Sessions and Cookies

A Django application depends on sessions and cookies whenever it needs to remember who a user is, what they have already done, and which preferences should survive from one request to the next. But, the challenge is that sessions and cookies are easy to treat as background details even though they sit directly inside the application's security boundary. A weak session configuration can increase the risk of session fixation, session theft, or accidental exposure over insecure transport.

Our objective in this recipe is to keep Django's session framework in place, but to shape it with a stronger current security posture so our authentication flow remains dependable in both development and production.

Choosing Session Backend and Lock Down Cookie Settings

A database-backed session store remains easy to understand and reliable, while the cached database backend is a good middle path when we want better performance but still want a database fallback. Once the backend is chosen, the real security posture comes from the cookie settings.

We should mark the session cookie as secure so the browser only sends it over HTTPS, keep it **HttpOnly** so ordinary client-side scripts cannot read it, and leave the SameSite policy explicit so cross-site requests do not receive the cookie casually. For most applications, **Lax** is a sensible starting point because it balances usability with protection against accidental cross-site submission. When the application is deployed behind a trusted reverse proxy that terminates **HTTPS**, the **SECURE_PROXY_SSL_HEADER** should also be set correctly so Django can recognize secure requests and apply secure-cookie behavior as intended.

```
# settings.py
SESSION_ENGINE = "django.contrib.sessions.backends.cached_db"
SESSION_COOKIE_SECURE = True
SESSION_COOKIE_HTTPONLY = True
SESSION_COOKIE_SAMESITE = "Lax"
SESSION_COOKIE_AGE = 60 * 60 * 24 * 14
SESSION_EXPIRE_AT_BROWSER_CLOSE = False
CSRF_COOKIE_SECURE = True
CSRF_COOKIE_SAMESITE = "Lax"
SECURE_PROXY_SSL_HEADER = ("HTTP_X_FORWARDED_PROTO", "https")
```

This above configuration gives us a practical balance. The cookie is protected in transit, hidden from ordinary JavaScript access, and scoped in a way that reduces risky cross-site behavior. We should also remember that login and logout flows already interact with session state in important ways. The Django's authentication system manages session use carefully, and our application should build on that instead of inventing its own parallel session logic.

Storing State and Cookie Attributes

A direct cookie can still be appropriate for a small anonymous preference, but when we set one ourselves we should be equally deliberate with its attributes. It is easy to call **set_cookie()** and forget that the cookie will otherwise inherit looser defaults than we might expect. And, this is why we should always think in terms of **expiry**, **secure**, **httponly**, and **samesite** when a cookie is written directly. The Django's response API supports all of those attributes directly, which means there is no reason to leave them unspecified when the meaning of the cookie is already known.

```
from django.http import HttpResponse
def set_theme(request):
    theme = request.GET.get("theme", "light")
```

```python
    request.session["theme"] = theme
    return HttpResponse(f"Theme set to {theme}")
def set_preference(request):
    response = HttpResponse("Preference saved")
    response.set_cookie(
        "preferred_language",
        "python",
        max_age=60 * 60 * 24 * 30,
        secure=True,
        httponly=False,
        samesite="Lax",
    )
    return response
```

This example keeps the server-tracked theme preference in the session while treating the language preference as a low-risk client cookie. The distinction matters because the two pieces of information have different sensitivity and different operational needs. A theme preference is fine in the session because it is tied to the user's server-side browsing state. A language hint can live in a direct cookie because it is not privileged information. The important point is that we decide where each value belongs and then set the corresponding cookie attributes deliberately rather than accepting whatever defaults happen to be in effect.

Maintaining Session Hygiene

A well-managed session system should feel invisible to the user and unsurprising to the developer. The browser stays signed in when it should, signed out when it should, and carries only the information needed to support the current experience.

```
python manage.py clearsessions
```

The Django's clearsessions command still exists for this maintenance step, and it remains a sensible part of periodic housekeeping for database-backed session stores.

The session framework still does the core work, but we now treat cookie attributes, proxy awareness, and session hygiene as part of the application's security design rather than as optional details that can be filled in later.

Recipe 7: Customizing Django Authentication Forms

Even when Django's built-in authentication forms are functionally correct, they rarely reflect the exact user experience, field layout, or messaging style that our app wants to present. We may want to add a remember-me option, style the fields more carefully, improve help text, use modern widget attributes, and render errors in a way that stays consistent with the rest of the project's forms.

So here, in this recipe, I will teach you to keep Django's built-in authentication behavior intact while moving to a more modern customization approach. We will learn to extend the forms we already have, use better widget attributes and rendering helpers, and allow the form layer own more of the presentation decisions instead of rebuilding them ad hoc in every template.

Adding Purposeful Fields and Widget Attributes

A login form that adds a remember-me option is a sensible example because it improves user control without interfering with authentication logic. We can extend **`AuthenticationForm`**, keep the built-in validation behavior, and then add our own field and widget-level improvements on top.

```
from django import forms
from django.contrib.auth.forms import AuthenticationForm
class CustomAuthenticationForm(AuthenticationForm):
    remember_me = forms.BooleanField(required=False,
label="Remember me")
    def __init__(self, *args, **kwargs):
        super().__init__(*args, **kwargs)
        self.fields["username"].widget.attrs.update(
            {
                "class": "form-control",
                "placeholder": "Enter our email",
                "autocomplete": "username",
            }
        )
        self.fields["password"].widget.attrs.update(
```

```
            {
                "class": "form-control",
                "placeholder": "Enter our password",
                "autocomplete": "current-password",
            }
        )
        self.fields["remember_me"].widget.attrs.update(
            {
                "class": "form-check-input",
            }
        )
```

In the above, the fields now advertise their purpose more clearly to the browser and to assistive tools, and the remember-me option is modeled directly in the form instead of being bolted on in the template. The same pattern works for registration forms, password change forms, and password reset request forms. We keep the built-in flow where it already serves us well and then improve the field layer where the application needs more control.

Using Boundfield-aware Rendering and Custom Login View

A modern form customization story should not stop with widget attributes. The form should also render labels, errors, and help text consistently, and Django's bound-field rendering helpers are a good fit for that. So here, instead of dumping the whole authentication form through **as_p**, we can render each field as a field group so the label, input, help text, and error output stay aligned.

```
from django.contrib.auth.views import LoginView
class CustomLoginView(LoginView):
    form_class = CustomAuthenticationForm
    template_name = "accounts/login.html"
    def form_valid(self, form):
        response = super().form_valid(form)
        if not form.cleaned_data.get("remember_me"):
            self.request.session.set_expiry(0)
        return response
```

```
<form method="post">
    {% csrf_token %}
    {{ form.non_field_errors }}
    {{ form.username.as_field_group }}
    {{ form.password.as_field_group }}
    {{ form.remember_me.as_field_group }}
    <button type="submit">Login</button>
</form>
```

This above pairing gives us a more modern and more maintainable authentication form flow. The view remains compact, the form owns the fields and widget behavior, and the template can render each field in a way that keeps labels and errors visible without repetitive manual markup. The result is a login experience that is cleaner for the user and easier for us to extend later. The same approach can be applied to UserCreationForm, password change forms, and password reset forms.

Recipe 8: Implementing Two-Factor Authentication

What two-factor authentication does is add an extra step to prove who you are, which makes it way harder for your account to be hacked, even if a password gets stolen or reused somewhere else. TOTP is still one of the best mainstream options because it avoids the weaknesses of SMS delivery and works well with authenticator apps that loads of users already know about. The idea here is to keep the core TOTP flow approachable while also checking the surrounding package compatibility.

Storing TOTP Secret and Generate Provisioning URI

The first step in a TOTP flow is to give each user who enables two-factor authentication a secret key that can be shared with an authenticator app. The user model or an adjacent profile model can store whether 2FA is enabled and the secret used for token generation. Once that secret exists, the application can generate a provisioning URI that authenticator apps understand. This URI is what powers the QR code the user scans during setup.

```
from django.db import models
from django.contrib.auth.models import AbstractUser
import pyotp
```

```
class CustomUser(AbstractUser):
    two_factor_enabled = models.BooleanField(default=False)
    otp_secret_key = models.CharField(max_length=100,
blank=True, default="")
    def generate_totp_secret(self):
        if not self.otp_secret_key:
            self.otp_secret_key = pyotp.random_base32()
            self.save(update_fields=["otp_secret_key"])
import pyotp
from django.contrib.auth.decorators import login_required
from django.shortcuts import render
@login_required
def setup_2fa(request):
    user = request.user
    user.generate_totp_secret()
    otp_uri =
pyotp.TOTP(user.otp_secret_key).provisioning_uri(
        name=user.email,
        issuer_name="GitforGits",
    )
    return render(
        request,
        "accounts/setup_2fa.html",
        {"otp_uri": otp_uri},
    )
```

The main thing we want to preserve in the above, is the idea that setup and verification are separate steps. The application first creates the secret, then shows the setup instructions, then confirms that the user can produce a valid code before marking 2FA as enabled. That sequencing is what keeps the feature both usable and safe.

Verifying Token as Second Authentication

Once setup exists, the login process needs a second verification step after the password is accepted. That second step should not replace the existing authentication flow. It should follow it. A user first proves knowledge of the password, then proves possession of the authenticator device by producing the time-based code.

```
import pyotp
from django.contrib import messages
from django.shortcuts import redirect, render
def verify_2fa_code(request):
    user = request.user
    token = request.POST.get("token", "").strip()
    totp = pyotp.TOTP(user.otp_secret_key)
    if totp.verify(token):
        user.two_factor_enabled = True
        user.save(update_fields=["two_factor_enabled"])
        messages.success(request, "Two-factor authentication
has been enabled.")
        return redirect("dashboard")
    messages.error(request, "The verification code is
invalid.")
    return render(request, "accounts/verify_2fa.html")
```

A successful verification can then complete the login flow or mark the session as fully two-factor-verified, depending on how the application separates "password accepted" from "*2FA accepted*". That separation is worth preserving because it keeps the user journey and the security model aligned. We know exactly what has been verified and when.

Recipe 9: Managing User Account Activation and Password Reset

Account activation and password reset are two of the most sensitive email-driven workflows in the entire application. The activation confirms that the email address belongs to the registering user, and the password reset gives a user a safe way back into the account without involving administrators or unsafe manual procedures.

Our aim in this recipe is, to rebuild both flows around task-backed email sending and Django's current email APIs. The activation flow should use a signed or tokenized link that marks the account verified only after the user proves control of the email address. The password reset flow should keep Django's trusted token-based mechanics while moving message delivery into a task-backed path so the browser receives a quick response even when email sending takes longer.

Building Activation Links with Tokens and Queue Email

A secure activation flow should tie the link to the user, keep it time-bounded, and avoid sending the email inline from the registration view. A clean pattern is to use Django's standard token tools together with the user's encoded identifier so the activation endpoint can recover the user securely and validate the token before marking **`email_verified`** as true. The email itself should be built through a helper that returns an EmailMultiAlternatives object, because that keeps both plain text and HTML variants in one structured message. The task layer can then deliver the email asynchronously using the task helper introduced earlier in the chapter.

```
from django.conf import settings
from django.contrib.auth.tokens import default_token_generator
from django.core.mail import EmailMultiAlternatives
from django.template.loader import render_to_string
from django.urls import reverse
from django.utils.http import urlsafe_base64_encode
from django.utils.encoding import force_bytes
def build_activation_email(user):
    uidb64 = urlsafe_base64_encode(force_bytes(user.pk))
    token = default_token_generator.make_token(user)
    activation_url = (
        f"{settings.SITE_URL}"
        f"{reverse('accounts:activate', kwargs={'uidb64':
uidb64, 'token': token})}"
    )
    context = {"user": user, "activation_url": activation_url}
    subject = "Activate our GitforGits account"
    text_body =
render_to_string("accounts/emails/activate.txt", context)
```

```
    html_body =
render_to_string("accounts/emails/activate.html", context)
    message = EmailMultiAlternatives(
        subject=subject,
        body=text_body,
        from_email=settings.DEFAULT_FROM_EMAIL,
        to=[user.email],
    )
    message.attach_alternative(html_body, "text/html")
    return message
from django.contrib import messages
from django.shortcuts import redirect, render
from .tasks import send_email_message_task
def register(request):
    if request.method == "POST":
        form = RegistrationForm(request.POST)
        if form.is_valid():
            user = form.save()
            message = build_activation_email(user)
            send_email_message_task.enqueue(
                subject=message.subject,
                body=message.body,
                from_email=message.from_email,
                to=message.to,
                alternatives=message.alternatives,
            )
            messages.success(request, "Check our email to
activate our account.")
            return redirect("accounts:login")
    else:
```

```
        form = RegistrationForm()
    return render(request, "accounts/register.html", {"form": form})
```

This above keeps the registration view lean and clear. It creates the account, builds the activation email, and enqueues the delivery task. The actual SMTP or backend delivery no longer blocks the browser, which makes the interaction smoother and reduces the temptation to hide email work behind slow inline helper calls.

Verifying Activation and Password Reset Flow

The activation view should decode the user id, load the user, and confirm the token before flipping the account into a verified state. The password reset flow should use Django's built-in reset views, because they already implement the token validation and multi-stage reset flow that users expect. What we do want to customize is the email delivery step, so the reset message follows the same task-backed pattern as the activation message.

```
from django.contrib.auth import get_user_model
from django.contrib.auth.tokens import default_token_generator
from django.shortcuts import get_object_or_404, redirect
from django.utils.encoding import force_str
from django.utils.http import urlsafe_base64_decode
User = get_user_model()
def activate_account(request, uidb64, token):
    user_id = force_str(urlsafe_base64_decode(uidb64))
    user = get_object_or_404(User, pk=user_id)
    if default_token_generator.check_token(user, token):
        user.email_verified = True
        user.is_active = True
        user.save(update_fields=["email_verified", "is_active"])
        return redirect("accounts:login")
    return redirect("accounts:activation_failed")
from django.conf import settings
from django.contrib.auth.forms import PasswordResetForm
```

```
from django.core.mail import EmailMultiAlternatives
class TaskBackedPasswordResetForm(PasswordResetForm):
    def send_mail(
        self,
        subject_template_name,
        email_template_name,
        context,
        from_email,
        to_email,
        html_email_template_name=None,
    ):
        subject = render_to_string(subject_template_name,
context).strip()
        body = render_to_string(email_template_name, context)
        message = EmailMultiAlternatives(
            subject=subject,
            body=body,
            from_email=from_email or
settings.DEFAULT_FROM_EMAIL,
            to=[to_email],
        )
        if html_email_template_name:
            html_body =
render_to_string(html_email_template_name, context)
            message.attach_alternative(html_body, "text/html")
        send_email_message_task.enqueue(
            subject=message.subject,
            body=message.body,
            from_email=message.from_email,
            to=message.to,
```

```
            alternatives=message.alternatives,
        )
from django.contrib.auth.views import PasswordResetView
class CustomPasswordResetView(PasswordResetView):
    form_class = TaskBackedPasswordResetForm
    email_template_name = "accounts/emails/password_reset.txt"
    html_email_template_name =
"accounts/emails/password_reset.html"
    subject_template_name =
"accounts/emails/password_reset_subject.txt"
    success_url = "/accounts/password-reset/done/"
```

This above arrangement gives us a complete and consistent account-recovery story. The activation view remains specific to account verification, while the password reset flow wisely continues to build on Django's own reset machinery rather than reinventing it. It is the strongest balance we can strike here.

Summary

Overall, we explored handling identity, access, and account security through a set of authentication and authorization patterns. We began by shaping a custom user model so the application could treat email as a central identity field and remain flexible enough for richer account behavior later. From there, we built advanced authentication flows that used email verification, passwordless login, and signed links to make account access both safer and more convenient. We also extended the chapter with a task-backed approach to authentication emails, which helped us treat verification and login messages as part of a structured workflow instead of as blocking actions inside a request.

We then worked through the access-control side of the chapter by using groups, permissions, and role-based rules to shape what different kinds of users could do inside our app. The social authentication and OAuth showed us how outside identity providers could be integrated without losing control over the application's own account system. After that, we strengthened the overall security posture through better session and cookie handling, more modern authentication form customization, and a clearer approach to two-factor authentication. We finished by rebuilding account activation and password reset flows around task-backed email sending and token-based verification, which gave us a more reliable and maintainable foundation for account recovery and ongoing user trust.

CHAPTER 7: DJANGO REST FRAMEWORK FOR APIS

Overview

This chapter will take us into the part of GitforGits where the application will begin to speak not only to browser pages, but also to other clients through a well-designed API. In this chapter, we will start setting up and configuring Django REST Framework for authentication, permissions, routing, and pagination. From there, we will build our first API endpoint and then move into serializers. As the chapter develops, we will also explore how more complex relationships can be represented through nested serializers.

The second half of the chapter will focus on the concerns of API reliability. We will apply authentication and permission rules, and then we will improve usability through pagination, filtering, and versioning patterns. After that, we will test and debug our API using DRF's own tools and supporting techniques. Finally, we will implement throttling and rate limiting so the API will handle traffic more fairly and remain more resilient under heavier demand.

Recipe 1: Setting up and Configuring DRF

In our app, once we want clients to interact with snippets, profiles, and related resources programmatically, we need an API layer that is clean, predictable, and easy to extend. The Django REST framework remains the natural choice because it integrates tightly with Django's models, authentication system, and request handling while still giving us enough structure to build APIs that grow well over time. The first task is not to rush into endpoints. The first task is to make sure REST framework is installed, registered, and configured in a way that matches the way we want the rest of the API chapter to behave.

So here, in this recipe, we will learn to add DRF to the project, establish a sensible baseline configuration for permissions and pagination, and wire up the early routing in a way that supports both API clients and the browsable API used during development and debugging.

Installing and Registering DRF

The cleanest way to start is to pin the chosen DRF version line. After installation, the Django needs to know about the framework, so we register **rest_framework** in **INSTALLED_APPS**.

```
python -m pip install "djangorestframework==3.17.1"
INSTALLED_APPS = [
    # Django apps
    "django.contrib.admin",
    "django.contrib.auth",
```

```
    "django.contrib.contenttypes",
    "django.contrib.sessions",
    "django.contrib.messages",
    "django.contrib.staticfiles",
    # Project apps
    "snippets",
    "accounts",
    # Third-party apps
    "rest_framework",
    "rest_framework.authtoken",
]
```

If the above installation and registration are vague here, every later example becomes slightly more fragile.

Setting Baseline

The DRF behaves best when the application sets a clear global baseline and then overrides that baseline only where individual endpoints truly need something different. In our app, a good starting point is to allow read-only access to unauthenticated users and require authentication for write operations. The pagination also deserves to be enabled early, because even small APIs grow quickly once the application becomes useful.

```
REST_FRAMEWORK = {
    "DEFAULT_PERMISSION_CLASSES": [

"rest_framework.permissions.IsAuthenticatedOrReadOnly",
    ],
    "DEFAULT_AUTHENTICATION_CLASSES": [
        "rest_framework.authentication.SessionAuthentication",
        "rest_framework.authentication.TokenAuthentication",
    ],
    "DEFAULT_PAGINATION_CLASS":
"rest_framework.pagination.PageNumberPagination",
```

```
    "PAGE_SIZE": 10,
}
```

This above setup gives us a practical default posture. The browsers and the browsable API can use session authentication, while API clients can later use token authentication. And, the read-only operations remain easy to explore, and write operations stay protected.

Adding API Routes and Authentication URLs

Next, we will add the browsable API login and logout routes to the project-level URLs. With it, we can either expose viewsets through routers or wire generic views directly.

```
from django.urls import include, path
from rest_framework.routers import DefaultRouter
from snippets.views import SnippetViewSet
router = DefaultRouter()
router.register("snippets", SnippetViewSet,
basename="snippet")
urlpatterns = [
    path("api/", include(router.urls)),
    path("api-auth/", include("rest_framework.urls",
namespace="rest_framework")),
]
```

This gives a stable API root and also keeps the browsable API practical during development. The login route is especially helpful when we want to test authenticated behavior through the browser without building a separate client first.

Running Migrations

Once the settings and URLs are in place, we will migrate the project so the **token-auth** tables exist and then run the server.

```
python manage.py migrate
python manage.py runserver
```

With this, you can easily establish a stable runway so the later serializer, authentication, testing, and throttling tasks can take off without having to fix the ground beneath them first.

Recipe 2: Building API View

Now that our DRF is set up, the first API view may be created. So here in this recipe, we will learn to create an API endpoint that is both easy to use and effective in retrieving a collection of code snippets.

Defining Serializer

Before creating the view, we need a way to convert our model instances into a format that can be easily rendered into JSON or XML for API responses. For this, we will define a serializer for our **`Snippet`** model in a new file **`serializers.py`** within our app:

```
from rest_framework import serializers
from .models import Snippet
class SnippetSerializer(serializers.ModelSerializer):
 class Meta:
 model = Snippet
 fields = ['id', 'title', 'code', 'created_at']
```

This serializer specifies which fields to include in the serialized representation of **`Snippet`** instances.

Creating View

Next, we will try to utilize DRF's viewsets or generic views to handle the logic of our API endpoint. For this, a generic **`ListAPIView`** can be used:

```
from rest_framework.generics import ListAPIView
from .models import Snippet
from .serializers import SnippetSerializer
class SnippetListView(ListAPIView):
 queryset = Snippet.objects.all()
 serializer_class = SnippetSerializer
```

This view automatically handles GET requests, returning a list of all **`Snippet`** instances in serialized form.

URL Configuration

Next, we will link our API view to a URL. For this, we will set up a **URLconf** in our app:

```
from django.urls import path
from .views import SnippetListView
urlpatterns = [
 path('snippets/', SnippetListView.as_view(), name='snippet-list'),
]
```

The above makes our snippet list API accessible at **/snippets/** which gives a straightforward endpoint for clients to interact with.

So, to access the endpoint, we just need to set up and launch the Django development server. And then, we can easily build scalable endpoints that retrieve application data efficiently by creating serializers and using DRF's built-in views.

Recipe 3: Working with Serializers for Complex Data

An API becomes more useful when it can represent the actual relationships inside the application instead of flattening everything into isolated records. Once an API needs to expose that connected structure, the serializer layer becomes one of the most important design points in the whole stack. In this recipe, we will learn to serialize nested data cleanly, and keep the relationship between parent and child objects understandable.

Defining Nested Serializers

A nested serializer works best when each layer has a clear job. The comment serializer should describe one comment. The snippet serializer should describe one snippet and nest the comments that belong to it. The user serializer should describe one user and nest the snippets that belong to that user. Once we frame the serializers that way, the JSON representation becomes much easier to reason about because it mirrors the structure of the domain itself.

```
from django.contrib.auth import get_user_model
from rest_framework import serializers
from .models import Comment, Snippet
User = get_user_model()
class CommentSerializer(serializers.ModelSerializer):
```

```
    author_email =
serializers.EmailField(source="author.email", read_only=True)
    class Meta:
        model = Comment
        fields = ["id", "body", "author_email", "created_at"]
class SnippetSerializer(serializers.ModelSerializer):
    comments = CommentSerializer(many=True, read_only=True)
    author_email =
serializers.EmailField(source="author.email", read_only=True)
    class Meta:
        model = Snippet
        fields = ["id", "title", "code", "created_at",
"author_email", "comments"]
class UserSerializer(serializers.ModelSerializer):
    snippets = SnippetSerializer(many=True, read_only=True)
    class Meta:
        model = User
        fields = ["id", "email", "snippets"]
```

Here, the user representation is now centered on email instead of assuming a username field exists or is primary. That small change matters because serializer examples should reinforce the project model rather than quietly drifting away from it.

Handling Nested Writes

The read-only nesting is quite an easiest part of the story. Whereas, the write operations need more care because DRF should not guess how deeply nested related objects should be created or updated. So here, if we want to create a snippet together with a batch of comments, then the serializer must own that workflow explicitly.

```
class WritableCommentSerializer(serializers.ModelSerializer):
    class Meta:
        model = Comment
        fields = ["body"]
```

```
class WritableSnippetSerializer(serializers.ModelSerializer):
    comments_data = WritableCommentSerializer(many=True,
write_only=True, required=False)
    class Meta:
        model = Snippet
        fields = ["id", "title", "code", "created_at",
"comments_data"]
        read_only_fields = ["id", "created_at"]
    def create(self, validated_data):
        comments_data = validated_data.pop("comments_data",
[])
        snippet = Snippet.objects.create(**validated_data)
        for comment_data in comments_data:
            Comment.objects.create(snippet=snippet,
**comment_data)
        return snippet
```

This pattern keeps the write path clear. The serializer is not pretending nested writes. It is stating exactly how related comment rows are created.

Readable Complex Serializers

A complex serializer can become hard to understand if it tries to do too much in one class. A good discipline is to separate read-oriented nested serializers from write-oriented serializers when the read shape and the write shape are meaningfully different. The read representation includes nested comments and author email. The write representation accepts **`comments_data`** explicitly and saves it deliberately. It keeps each serializer focused and prevents one class from becoming a confusing mixture of display logic and write orchestration.

Overall, the nested serializers still give the API richer data representation, but the code now matches the custom-user approach and treats nested writes with the care they actually require.

Recipe 4: Implementing Authentication and Permissions in APIs

An API needs a clear answer to two questions on every request. One is, ***who is making this***

request, and the other is, ***what are they allowed to do with the object or endpoint they are trying to reach?*** Our app cannot allow every client to create, edit, or delete snippets freely. Some actions should require authentication, and some write operations should be limited to the snippet owner or an administrative user.

So here, in this recipe, we will learn to wire token authentication correctly, shape a useful object-level permission class, and make sure snippet ownership is enforced consistently during both creation and modification.

Configuring Token Authentication

If we teach **TokenAuthentication**, then the project must also include **rest_framework.authtoken** and migrate it. This part is easy to miss, but without it the token tables do not exist and the example becomes incomplete.

```
INSTALLED_APPS = [
    # ...
    "rest_framework",
    "rest_framework.authtoken",
]
REST_FRAMEWORK = {
    "DEFAULT_AUTHENTICATION_CLASSES": [
        "rest_framework.authentication.TokenAuthentication",
    ],
    "DEFAULT_PERMISSION_CLASSES": [
"rest_framework.permissions.IsAuthenticatedOrReadOnly",
    ],
}
python manage.py migrate
```

in the above, once the app is installed, the DRF can use token authentication in the global settings or on specific views. After that, each user needs a token. We can create it manually, at registration time, or through a **post_save** signal.

```
from django.conf import settings
from django.db.models.signals import post_save
```

```
from django.dispatch import receiver
from rest_framework.authtoken.models import Token
@receiver(post_save, sender=settings.AUTH_USER_MODEL)
def create_auth_token(sender, instance=None, created=False,
**kwargs):
    if created:
        Token.objects.create(user=instance)
```

In the above script, the user can sign in through the site, receive or retrieve a token, and then supply that token in the **`Authorization: Token`** ... header for API access.

Defining Object-level Permission

The DRF's permission system works at both the view and object level, but object-level checks only happen when the view actually retrieves an object. This is why a custom permission class is so useful for update and delete flows.

```
from rest_framework import permissions
class IsOwnerOrReadOnly(permissions.BasePermission):
    def has_object_permission(self, request, view, obj):
        if request.method in permissions.SAFE_METHODS:
            return True
        return obj.owner == request.user
```

This above matches our app's use case well because reading snippets may be public or semi-public, while modification should remain with the owner. The important part is that we use the same ownership field consistently in the model and in the view logic. If the snippet model calls that field owner, then the permission class should do the same. If the model calls it author, then the entire example should align with that field name.

Applying Permission in View

A permission class alone is not enough for creation, because the object-level permission checks do not automatically decide who the object owner should be when the object does not exist yet. The view must take responsibility for that by setting the owner during creation.

```
from rest_framework.authentication import TokenAuthentication
```

```
from rest_framework.generics import ListCreateAPIView,
RetrieveUpdateDestroyAPIView
from .models import Snippet
from .permissions import IsOwnerOrReadOnly
from .serializers import SnippetSerializer
class SnippetListCreateView(ListCreateAPIView):
    queryset = Snippet.objects.all()
    serializer_class = SnippetSerializer
    authentication_classes = [TokenAuthentication]
    permission_classes =
[permissions.IsAuthenticatedOrReadOnly]
    def perform_create(self, serializer):
        serializer.save(owner=self.request.user)
class SnippetDetailView(RetrieveUpdateDestroyAPIView):
    queryset = Snippet.objects.all()
    serializer_class = SnippetSerializer
    authentication_classes = [TokenAuthentication]
    permission_classes = [IsOwnerOrReadOnly]
```

In the above, the authentication identifies the caller. The view-level permissions shape the broad access rule. The object-level permissions protect modification. And, the **`perform_create()`** ensures ownership is assigned at the moment of creation. So here, nothing is left implicit.

Overall, the API accepts authenticated requests through token auth, allows read access more broadly, restricts writes, and assigns ownership at creation time. It is a complete pattern. Once we understand it for snippets, we can apply the same logic to comments, profiles, and other API-backed resources later in the project.

Recipe 5: Customizing Pagination and Filtering

An API becomes harder to use once it starts returning too much data at once or gives clients no reliable way to narrow the result set. Hence, the pagination and filtering are therefore not luxuries. They are part of making the API practical and stable for us.

So, in this recipe, we will try to keep pagination customizable while modernizing filtering to fit the current DRF style better.

Keeping Pagination Explicit

A custom pagination class remains a good way to shape the response payload. A client often needs the next and previous links, the current page, and the total page count in one predictable structure. This makes pagination easier to consume than a bare list of objects with little context about where the current slice sits in the larger result set.

```
from rest_framework.pagination import PageNumberPagination
from rest_framework.response import Response
class CustomPagination(PageNumberPagination):
    page_size = 10
    page_size_query_param = "page_size"
    max_page_size = 100
    def get_paginated_response(self, data):
        return Response(
            {
                "links": {
                    "next": self.get_next_link(),
                    "previous": self.get_previous_link(),
                },
                "total_pages": self.page.paginator.num_pages,
                "current_page": self.page.number,
                "page_size": self.get_page_size(self.request),
                "results": data,
            }
        )
```

The above makes the payload slightly cleaner and more explicit. The client can navigate through the result set with less guesswork, and the API response becomes easier to consume in both browser-based and external clients.

Using Django-Filter for Filtering

For filtering, the modern sweet spot is to let **`DjangoFilterBackend`** handle straightforward equality-based query parameters. It keeps the view compact and makes the filterable fields obvious. It also gives us a clean migration path later if we decide to move from simple field lists to explicit **FilterSet** classes.

```
python -m pip install django-filter
INSTALLED_APPS = [
    # ...
    "django_filters",
]
REST_FRAMEWORK = {
    "DEFAULT_FILTER_BACKENDS": [
        "django_filters.rest_framework.DjangoFilterBackend",
    ],
    "DEFAULT_PAGINATION_CLASS":
"snippets.pagination.CustomPagination",
    "PAGE_SIZE": 10,
}
from django_filters.rest_framework import DjangoFilterBackend
from rest_framework.generics import ListAPIView
from .models import Snippet
from .serializers import SnippetSerializer
from .pagination import CustomPagination
class SnippetListView(ListAPIView):
    queryset = Snippet.objects.all().order_by("-created_at")
    serializer_class = SnippetSerializer
    pagination_class = CustomPagination
    filter_backends = [DjangoFilterBackend]
    filterset_fields = ["language", "owner"]
```

The above is easier to extend than the earlier hand-written **get_queryset()** approach for simple filters. A request such as **?language=python** or **?owner=12** now maps directly to the declared filter fields. The intent is clearer, and the view stays focused on the endpoint rather than on repetitive query-parameter plumbing.

Once you understand **DjangoFilterBackend** and **filterset_fields**, you can graduate naturally to more advanced filter classes and queryset overrides.

Recipe 6: API Versioning Best Practices

There will inevitably be updates to current endpoints or the introduction of new features. But apps and consumers depending on our API might get disrupted by such changes. To handle these changes with grace, versioning strategies need to be implemented.

Configuring Versioning in DRF

The DRF supports various versioning schemes out of the box, including URL path versioning, query parameter versioning, and header versioning. The choice of scheme depends on our API's specific needs and the preferences of its consumers. The URL path versioning (**/api/v1/**) is one of the most straightforward and commonly used methods.

At first, we will update **DEFAULT_VERSIONING_CLASS** in **settings.py** to make use of **rest_framework.versioning.URLPathVersioning**. Also, we will specify a default version and allowed versions:

```
REST_FRAMEWORK = {
 'DEFAULT_VERSIONING_CLASS':
'rest_framework.versioning.URLPathVersioning',
 'DEFAULT_VERSION': 'v1',
 'ALLOWED_VERSIONS': ['v1', 'v2'],
 'VERSION_PARAM': 'version',
}
```

Adapting URLs and Views

Here, we will now modify our **urls.py** to include the version in the URL path. The DRF's **path** function supports versioning directly:

```
from django.urls import path, include
from rest_framework.routers import DefaultRouter
from . import views
# Assuming you have a router set up for our views
```

```
router = DefaultRouter()
router.register(r'snippets', views.SnippetViewSet)
urlpatterns = [
 path('api/<version>/', include(router.urls)),
]
```

In views, we can access the version of request via **`reverse(..., request=request)`** and adjust the behavior accordingly.

Recipe 7: Testing DRF Applications

An API chapter without testing leaves too much to hope. Once our app starts exposing snippets, authenticated write endpoints, and protected resources, we need a dependable way to verify that responses, permissions, and payloads behave the way the design expects.

So here in this recipe, we will learn to keep the project's tests clear, realistic, and close to the way clients actually interact with the API, while still making it easy for us to force authentication when a test is focused on the endpoint behavior rather than the mechanics of login.

Using APIClient as API Test Client

The DRF's **`APIClient`** remains the most practical default testing tool for ordinary endpoint tests. It actually mirrors the Django's test client while understanding API-style requests, JSON payloads, and authentication helpers. Using it, we can write tests that feel like real client interactions without having to build requests by hand for every case.

```
from django.urls import reverse
from rest_framework import status
from rest_framework.test import APIClient
def test_snippet_list():
    client = APIClient()
    url = reverse("snippet-list")
    response = client.get(url)
    assert response.status_code == status.HTTP_200_OK
```

This above test is small, but it does important work. It verifies that the endpoint resolves, that the list route is accessible, and that the API is responding with the expected status code.

Aligning Test User Creation with Custom User Model

Next, instead of importing **django.contrib.auth.models.User**, we make use of **get_user_model()**, so the tests remain correct even when the project uses an email-based custom user model.

```
import pytest
from django.contrib.auth import get_user_model
from django.urls import reverse
from rest_framework import status
from rest_framework.test import APIClient
from .models import Snippet
User = get_user_model()
@pytest.mark.django_db
def test_create_snippet_authenticated():
    client = APIClient()
    user = User.objects.create_user(
        email="test@gitforgits.com",
        password="testpassword123",
    )
    client.force_authenticate(user=user)
    url = reverse("snippet-list")
    data = {
        "title": "Test Snippet",
        "code": 'print("hello, world")',
        "language": "python",
    }
    response = client.post(url, data, format="json")
    assert response.status_code == status.HTTP_201_CREATED
    assert Snippet.objects.filter(title="Test Snippet",
owner=user).exists()
```

The above test is about whether an authenticated user can create a snippet through the endpoint, not about whether the login flow itself works. And, this is why forcing authentication is appropriate here. It lets the test concentrate on the behavior under inspection.

Testing Permissions and Failure Paths

A strong API test suite should also check that unauthorized actions are rejected, not only that happy-path requests succeed. So, the fastest way to trust an ownership rule is to test both the owner case and the non-owner case.

```
@pytest.mark.django_db
def test_update_snippet_denied_for_non_owner():
    client = APIClient()
    owner =
User.objects.create_user(email="owner@gitforgits.com",
password="ownerpass")
    other_user =
User.objects.create_user(email="other@gitforgits.com",
password="otherpass")
    snippet = Snippet.objects.create(
        owner=owner,
        title="Locked Snippet",
        code="print('secure')",
        language="python",
    )
    client.force_authenticate(user=other_user)
    url = reverse("snippet-detail", args=[snippet.id])
    response = client.patch(url, {"title": "Modified"},
format="json")
    assert response.status_code == status.HTTP_403_FORBIDDEN
```

This above kind of test is where the value of API testing becomes obvious. We are not merely checking that the endpoint exists. We are checking that the authorization policy really behaves the way the application promises. That matters much more in practice than a long suite of shallow status-code checks, because the project's real trust boundary lives in these permission rules.

The best API tests stay close to the way the API is actually consumed. That means using JSON payloads where the endpoint expects JSON, using real route reversing, and checking meaningful response content rather than only status codes. It also means resisting the temptation to bypass too much of the request flow.

Recipe 8: Debugging DRF Applications

If we want to keep our service up and running smoothly, find and fix problems fast, and keep our users happy, we need debugging tactics that work. The interplay between serializers, views, authentication systems, and third-party clients in DRF applications, like in any complex system, can make debugging a unique difficulty.

Using Django Debug Toolbar

The Django Debug offers detailed insights into the SQL queries generated by our views, performance data, request and response headers, and more.

```
INSTALLED_APPS += ['debug_toolbar']
MIDDLEWARE +=
['debug_toolbar.middleware.DebugToolbarMiddleware']
DEBUG_TOOLBAR_CONFIG = {
 'SHOW_TOOLBAR_CALLBACK': lambda request: True, # Forces the
toolbar to show for DRF views
}
```

To use the toolbar with DRF, we shall first confirm that the API views are capable of rendering HTML responses or temporarily switch to a standard Django view while debugging.

Configuring Django Logging

If you've got logging set up right, you can get some pretty useful info about how your app's behaving. For example, you can see all the requests and responses, and any system errors. The Django logging framework is really flexible, so we can log messages at different levels of severity and send logs to different places (console, file, email, etc.).

```
LOGGING = {
 'version': 1,
 'disable_existing_loggers': False,
 'handlers': {
 'console': {
```

```
 'class': 'logging.StreamHandler',
 },
 },
 'loggers': {
 'django': {
 'handlers': ['console'],
 'level': 'DEBUG',
 },
 },
}
```

There are tools like Postman and cURL which can simulate client requests to our API to methodically test and debug various API endpoints. They are quite useful for debugging authentication issues, testing header configurations, and replicating client-reported errors.

Also, there's a way to customise DRF's exception handling to catch and log exceptions or to modify the response data for errors. It's got these DRF hooks for custom exception handling, which you can use to add debugging info to error responses or integrate with error tracking services.

Recipe 9: Implementing API Throttling and Rate Limiting

Once an API becomes useful, it also becomes vulnerable to overuse. That overuse does not always come from malicious intent. A poorly written client, an overly aggressive polling loop, or one endpoint that attracts heavy traffic can all create load that hurts the experience for everyone else. The throttling helps us control that. It is not a full security solution against determined abuse, but it is a valuable application-level policy tool for fair usage and stable operation.

So, in this recipe, we will keep the global throttle settings simple and then show you a clearer custom throttle path for more sensitive operations such as snippet creation.

Setting Global Baseline Throttle Policy

Well, a good default policy distinguishes between anonymous and authenticated traffic. An anonymous client usually deserve a tighter limit, while an authenticated user can often have a broader quota. The DRF already provides **`AnonRateThrottle`** and **`UserRateThrottle`** for this baseline.

```
REST_FRAMEWORK = {
    "DEFAULT_THROTTLE_CLASSES": [
        "rest_framework.throttling.AnonRateThrottle",
        "rest_framework.throttling.UserRateThrottle",
    ],
    "DEFAULT_THROTTLE_RATES": {
        "anon": "100/day",
        "user": "1000/day",
    },
}
```

The above script gives the API a practical floor of protection. The anonymous traffic cannot hammer the service indefinitely, and authenticated traffic also stays within a defined range.

Custom Throttle for Write-Heavy Endpoints

A clearer modern path is either to use **`ScopedRateThrottle`** for endpoint groups or to subclass **`UserRateThrottle`** or **`SimpleRateThrottle`** cleanly for a specific action. For snippet creation, we can define a dedicated scope and give it its own rate as shown below:

```
from rest_framework.throttling import UserRateThrottle
class SnippetCreateThrottle(UserRateThrottle):
    scope = "snippet_create"
REST_FRAMEWORK = {
    "DEFAULT_THROTTLE_CLASSES": [
        "rest_framework.throttling.AnonRateThrottle",
        "rest_framework.throttling.UserRateThrottle",
    ],
    "DEFAULT_THROTTLE_RATES": {
        "anon": "100/day",
        "user": "1000/day",
        "snippet_create": "10/hour",
    },
```

```
}
```

The above is quite cleaner than the earlier example because we let DRF's existing per-user throttling behavior do most of the work instead of writing our own cache-key logic prematurely.

Applying Custom Throttle

Once the custom throttle exists, we then attach it to the write-heavy endpoint. A list-and-create view is quite a natural example because the listing can use the broader default rate, while creation may deserve the additional tighter limit.

```
from rest_framework.generics import ListCreateAPIView
from rest_framework.throttling import UserRateThrottle
from .models import Snippet
from .serializers import SnippetSerializer
from .throttling import SnippetCreateThrottle
class SnippetListCreateView(ListCreateAPIView):
    queryset = Snippet.objects.all()
    serializer_class = SnippetSerializer
    throttle_classes = [UserRateThrottle,
SnippetCreateThrottle]
    def perform_create(self, serializer):
        serializer.save(owner=self.request.user)
```

The above tells DRF to apply both the general authenticated-user throttle and the narrower snippet-creation policy. That creates a layered throttle story, which is often exactly what we want for write operations. A client may still browse the API within one quota, but actual resource creation gets tighter control.

Summary

Overall, we learned to use Django REST Framework through a structured and maintainable API layer. We began by setting up and configuring DRF so the project could serve API endpoints with sensible defaults for permissions, authentication, and pagination. We built the first API view and learned how serializers transformed model instances into API-friendly representations. We then worked through complex serializers for nested relationships so users, snippets, and related records could be represented clearly without losing the shape of the underlying data.

Later, we improved API usability and operational stability by customizing pagination and filtering so clients could retrieve data in a more controlled and readable way. We also looked at versioning strategies, which showed us how API evolution could be managed without breaking existing consumers. After that, we focused on testing and debugging, where we used DRF's testing tools, browsable API, and supporting diagnostics to keep the API dependable and easier to troubleshoot. Finally, throttling and rate limiting helped us shape fair usage rules and protect the service from excessive traffic.

CHAPTER 8: TESTING, SECURITY, AND DEPLOYMENT

Overview

This chapter aims at developing correctness, deployment readiness, and security of our app. We will begin by working with unit tests so we can confirm that important parts of the project will continue to behave correctly as the codebase changes. After that, we will move into automated testing, where we will shape a workflow that will run checks consistently under Python 3.12 during local development and through shared CI pipelines. From there, we will shift into production preparation by building a clearer settings pattern, separating development assumptions from deployment realities, and following an operational checklist.

Later, we will move into deployment and runtime hardening. We will learn to deploy Django in a more modern, ASGI-aware way, how reverse proxies and supervised processes will fit into that deployment story, and how static assets and user-uploaded media will be handled through a cleaner STORAGES model. We will then secure traffic with HTTPS and SSL certificates, and from that secure transport baseline we will continue into browser-side protections through Content Security Policy. By the end, we can be sure of testing, deployment, storage, HTTPS, and CSP for our app working together for production environment.

Recipe 1: Writing Unit Tests

The more time that goes by, the more important it is to make sure its features are stable and reliable. One way to make sure specific parts work right is to do some unit testing. The **`unittest`** module is a built-in Python library for implementing unit tests, and it makes it really easy to write unit tests in Django. It let developers create test cases that are separate, repeatable and not affected by outside influences, so you can be sure the application will work as expected in different situations.

Setting up Test Environment

The **`unittest`** module provides a rich set of tools for constructing and running tests. It supports test automation, sharing of setup and shutdown code for tests, aggregation of tests into collections, and independence of the tests from reporting framework. The basic building blocks of a unit test are test cases, which are Python classes that inherit from **`unittest.TestCase`**.

To start with, we will create a file named **`test_models.py`** in the app's tests directory to test our models.

Writing Unit Test

We will begin with testing the Snippet model. We will try to verify that creating and saving a new Snippet instance works as expected.

```
from django.test import TestCase
```

```
from .models import Snippet
class SnippetModelTest(TestCase):
 def setUp(self):
 # Setup run before every test method.
 Snippet.objects.create(title="Hello World",
code="print('Hello, world!')")
 def test_snippet_content(self):
 # Test retrieving a snippet and verifying its content.
 snippet = Snippet.objects.get(title="Hello World")
 expected_object_name = f'{snippet.title}'
 expected_object_code = f'{snippet.code}'
 self.assertEqual(expected_object_name, "Hello World")
 self.assertEqual(expected_object_code, "print('Hello,
world!')")
```

This test case **SnippetModelTest** contains two test methods. One is **setUp**, which initializes a Snippet instance before each test, and the other is **test_snippet_content**, which asserts that the snippet's title and code are correctly stored and retrieved.

Running Tests

Next, we will now execute the tests:

```
python manage.py test
```

After this, the Django will discover tests under any file named with a **tests.py** pattern or files in a tests directory and execute them using the unittest framework. It prints the results to the console after each test run. If the Django encounters an error, then it produces comprehensive output that assists in identifying the cause of the problem. The developers may build a more solid and reliable platform by thoroughly testing each component to find and fix bugs faster.

Recipe 2: Automate Testing

Well, running tests only when we remember to do so becomes one of the easiest ways to let regressions slip into the main codebase. A small application may tolerate that for a while, but once models, forms, authentication, API endpoints, and deployment checks begin to move together, the cost of missed breakage rises quickly. And, this is why test automation matters. It moves testing from an occasional developer habit into a dependable part of the workflow.

In this recipe, we will practice to automate the test run in two complementary places. First, we will place a lightweight guard close to development so obvious failures are caught before code is committed. Then we will move the shared project verification into GitHub Actions so every push and pull request runs the same test workflow under Python 3.12.

Adding Local Guard for Fast Feedback

A local automation step is useful because it catches breakage close to the moment we make it. The goal is not to replace the shared CI workflow. The goal is to stop simple failures before they ever leave the developer's machine. Since we are using a virtual environment 'venv', we can activate it first and then run the tests through the same interpreter. This small detail matters because a test script that silently uses the wrong Python interpreter can be worse than no automation at all.

```
#!/bin/sh
. venv/bin/activate
python --version
python manage.py test
if [ $? -ne 0 ]; then
  echo "Tests failed. Commit aborted."
  exit 1
fi
```

We then save it and make it executable:

```
.git/hooks/pre-commit
chmod +x .git/hooks/pre-commit
```

This gives us immediate value because it catches failing tests before they are committed. It also encourages a healthier development rhythm. We write or change code, we commit, and the test suite becomes part of that rhythm instead of a separate, optional activity we may remember later. Still, this hook is only local. It is not shared by default through the repository, and it does not prove that the code works in the clean environment used by the rest of the team.

Creating Shared Github Actions Workflow

A shared automation workflow should run whenever code is pushed or proposed through a pull request. This is where GitHub Actions fits naturally because it gives us a repository-level CI pipeline that can build the environment, install dependencies, and run the tests in a clean runner every time.

So now, we will create this file:

```
.github/workflows/django-ci.yml
```

And, we will now add the following workflow:

```
name: Django CI
on:
  push:
  pull_request:
jobs:
  test:
    runs-on: ubuntu-latest
    steps:
      - name: Check out repository
        uses: actions/checkout@v4
      - name: Set up Python 3.12
        uses: actions/setup-python@v5
        with:
          python-version: "3.12"
          cache: "pip"
      - name: Install dependencies
        run: |
          python -m pip install --upgrade pip
          pip install -r requirements.txt
      - name: Run Django system checks
        run: |
          python manage.py check
      - name: Run test suite
        run: |
```

```
        python manage.py test
```

This workflow is intentionally focused. It checks out the code, installs Python 3.12, installs dependencies, runs Django's system checks, and then runs the test suite. Here, a pull request now has to pass the same clean run every time, which reduces the risk that a developer's local environment accidentally masked a problem.

This recipe we built is not a dead-end script. It is a durable starting point for the rest of the project's testing lifecycle. The important thing is to keep the workflow readable and tied to the actual development stack.

Recipe 3: Setting up Production Environment

A production environment should have explicit hosts, secret management through environment variables, database and cache settings that match the deployed infrastructure, safe cookie behavior, predictable static and media handling, and a checklist we can run before launch with confidence.

The goal of this recipe is to shape a production-ready pattern that we can apply whether the final deployment lands on AWS, another cloud provider, or a managed platform.

Splitting Production Configuration

A production environment works best when it is expressed deliberately instead of being patched into the same settings file that local development uses. At minimum, production should get its **SECRET_KEY**, **DEBUG**, **ALLOWED_HOSTS**, and database configuration from environment variables rather than from hard-coded placeholders.

```
# settings/production.py
from .base import *
import os
DEBUG = False
SECRET_KEY = os.environ["DJANGO_SECRET_KEY"]
ALLOWED_HOSTS = os.environ.get("DJANGO_ALLOWED_HOSTS",
"gitforgits.com").split(",")
CSRF_TRUSTED_ORIGINS = os.environ.get(
    "DJANGO_CSRF_TRUSTED_ORIGINS",
    "https://gitforgits.com,https://www.gitforgits.com",
).split(",")
```

```
DATABASES = {
    "default": {
        "ENGINE": "django.db.backends.postgresql",
        "NAME": os.environ["DB_NAME"],
        "USER": os.environ["DB_USER"],
        "PASSWORD": os.environ["DB_PASSWORD"],
        "HOST": os.environ["DB_HOST"],
        "PORT": os.environ.get("DB_PORT", "5432"),
        "CONN_MAX_AGE": 60,
    }
}
```

This immediately removes several common production risks. The secret key is no longer stored inside the repository. The debug mode is disabled. The allowed hosts are explicit rather than accidental, and the database settings no longer assume a local development database. Once the settings are environment-driven, the rest of the deployment story becomes easier because the same codebase can move between environments without editing source files every time a hostname, credential, or database endpoint changes.

Applying Security and Operational Settings

A production environment should also carry security defaults that browsers and proxies can trust. Secure cookies, **HttpOnly** session handling, and explicit **SameSite** behavior are part of that. So are HTTPS-related settings such as **SECURE_SSL_REDIRECT** and **HSTS** when the deployment is truly HTTPS-only. If the application is behind a proxy that terminates **TLS**, **SECURE_PROXY_SSL_HEADER** should be configured so Django knows the original request was secure.

We also need a logging configuration, a predictable static and media plan, and a place for error reporting. The Django's deployment checklist is helpful precisely because it treats these items as part of the normal definition of deployment, not as later extras we might remember only after something goes wrong.

```
SESSION_COOKIE_SECURE = True
SESSION_COOKIE_HTTPONLY = True
SESSION_COOKIE_SAMESITE = "Lax"
CSRF_COOKIE_SECURE = True
```

```
CSRF_COOKIE_SAMESITE = "Lax"
SECURE_SSL_REDIRECT = True
SECURE_PROXY_SSL_HEADER = ("HTTP_X_FORWARDED_PROTO", "https")
SECURE_HSTS_SECONDS = 31536000
SECURE_HSTS_INCLUDE_SUBDOMAINS = True
SECURE_HSTS_PRELOAD = True
STORAGES = {
    "default": {
        "BACKEND":
"django.core.files.storage.FileSystemStorage",
    },
    "staticfiles": {
        "BACKEND":
"django.contrib.staticfiles.storage.StaticFilesStorage",
    },
}
LOGGING = {
    "version": 1,
    "disable_existing_loggers": False,
    "handlers": {
        "console": {"class": "logging.StreamHandler"},
    },
    "root": {
        "handlers": ["console"],
        "level": "INFO",
    },
}
```

The above settings turn the production configuration into something concrete. The cookies are secured, HTTPS behavior is explicit, storage roles are declared, and logging has at least one usable output instead of disappearing into silence. Now here, depending on the deployment, we may later replace the default storage backend or forward logs into a managed system.

Running Operational Checklist

The Django's **check --deploy** is extremely useful here because it turns a vague idea of production readiness into a concrete system check run. We should use it before launch and also after major settings changes.

```
python manage.py migrate
python manage.py collectstatic
python manage.py check --deploy
```

The operational checklist should also include migrations, static asset collection, environment variable verification, process supervision, and reverse proxy validation. These are not glamorous tasks, but they are the ones that determine whether the deployment feels stable from the first request. The reason this matters so much is that production readiness is the combination of settings, runtime services, and a habit of verifying them together. The Django's system check framework explicitly includes deployment-specific warnings such as missing **ALLOWED_HOSTS**, which makes it a practical final gate before we go live.

Overall, this recipe took us to the deeper thing the project actually needs, which is a production settings pattern and operational checklist we can trust. Once they are in place, the rest of deployment becomes easier, because the application already knows how it expects to behave in production.

Recipe 4: Deploying Apps to Production

A deployment is about shaping the runtime path from version-controlled code to installed dependencies, migrated database, collected static assets, supervised application process, and reverse proxy entry point. Our app deserves an ASGI-aware framing here, because Django 6.0 supports both WSGI and ASGI, and Django's own deployment overview now describes ASGI as the asynchronous-friendly standard for future-facing deployments. That does not mean every Django project must immediately become deeply asynchronous.

Our goal in this recipe is therefore to keep the deployment path practical and familiar while modernizing it around a clean ASGI entry point using asgi.py, a supervised application server, and Nginx as the reverse proxy.

Preparing Server, Code, and Python Runtime

To start with, we pull the latest code, activate the project environment, install dependencies from the locked requirements file, and then run the standard Django deployment checks.

```
cd /srv/gitforgits
git pull origin main
source venv/bin/activate
python --version
pip install -r requirements.txt
python manage.py migrate
python manage.py collectstatic --noinput
python manage.py check --deploy
```

This sequence gives us a dependable transition from code update to production validation. The **python --version** check is worth keeping visible because it confirms we are running the same runtime version throughout this learning. The **check --deploy** step is equally important because it validates the environment through Django's own deployment-aware checks before we restart the application process.

Running Django through ASGI

Since Django ships with **asgi.py** by default and supports ASGI deployment officially, a clean deployment path is to run the application through Uvicorn under **systemd**.

```
python -m uvicorn gitforgits.asgi:application --host 127.0.0.1
--port 8001
```

Next, we then create a **systemd** service file:

```
[Unit]
Description=GitforGits ASGI application
After=network.target
[Service]
User=www-data
Group=www-data
WorkingDirectory=/srv/gitforgits
Environment="DJANGO_SETTINGS_MODULE=gitforgits.settings.produc
tion"
```

```
ExecStart=/srv/gitforgits/venv/bin/python -m uvicorn
gitforgits.asgi:application --host 127.0.0.1 --port 8001
Restart=always
[Install]
WantedBy=multi-user.target
```

And then, we enable and start it:

```
sudo systemctl daemon-reload
sudo systemctl enable gitforgits
sudo systemctl start gitforgits
sudo systemctl status gitforgits
```

It gives us a robust process lifecycle. The Uvicorn serves the ASGI application, **systemd** supervises it, and the application becomes a managed service rather than a shell process we hope remains alive after we disconnect.

Placing Nginx in Deployment

A reverse proxy still belongs in front of the application server because it handles client connections, request forwarding, static file paths, headers, and TLS termination much more effectively than the application server itself should. The Nginx remains a solid fit for this role.

```
server {
    listen 80;
    server_name gitforgits.com www.gitforgits.com;
    location / {
        proxy_pass http://127.0.0.1:8001;
        proxy_set_header Host $host;
        proxy_set_header X-Forwarded-Proto $scheme;
        proxy_set_header X-Real-IP $remote_addr;
        proxy_set_header X-Forwarded-For
$proxy_add_x_forwarded_for;
    }
    location /static/ {
```

```
        alias /srv/gitforgits/staticfiles/;
    }
    location /media/ {
        alias /srv/gitforgits/media/;
    }
}
sudo nginx -t
sudo systemctl reload nginx
```

Once the proxy is configured, the final deployment steps are to test the Nginx syntax, reload the proxy, and verify that the security groups or firewall rules expose only the intended ports.

The whole process of deployment is still about updating code, installing dependencies, migrating data, collecting static files, and reloading services. The difference is that the runtime framing now matches Django's current deployment direction more closely by acknowledging ASGI as the forward-looking standard and placing a supervised ASGI server behind Nginx.

Recipe 5: Managing Static Files in Production

Once moving into production, the static files stop being a small convenience and become part of the application's delivery pipeline. The CSS, JavaScript, icons, and layout images need to be collected, versioned, and served consistently, while the user-uploaded media must remain separate because it is not part of the deployable codebase. The static assets belong to the application and should be collected into a production-ready location. And, the media files belong to users and should be stored through the default file storage without being treated as though they were build artifacts.

This recipe is meant to shape a production static-files path that is predictable, cache-friendly, and aligned with the storage.

Separating Production Static Assets

The first discipline of production file handling is to stop thinking of all public files as one category. The Django's deployment checklist makes a very clear distinction by warning that media files are user-controlled and should never be interpreted by the web server as executable code, while the staticfiles app expects deployable assets to be collected and served through the storage configured for staticfiles. In general, a production settings layout should therefore declare **STATIC_URL**, **STATIC_ROOT**, **MEDIA_URL**, and **MEDIA_ROOT**, then use **STORAGES** to make different responsibilities explicit.

```
from pathlib import Path
BASE_DIR = Path(__file__).resolve().parent.parent
STATIC_URL = "/static/"
STATIC_ROOT = BASE_DIR / "staticfiles"
MEDIA_URL = "/media/"
MEDIA_ROOT = BASE_DIR / "media"
STORAGES = {
    "default": {
        "BACKEND":
"django.core.files.storage.FileSystemStorage",
    },
    "staticfiles": {
        "BACKEND":
"django.contrib.staticfiles.storage.ManifestStaticFilesStorage
",
    },
}
```

This above configuration does three important things at once:

- It gives collected static assets a dedicated destination,
- It preserves a separate media location for uploaded files, and
- It upgrades production static delivery to **ManifestStaticFilesStorage**, which fingerprints asset filenames and helps long-lived browser caching work safely because changed assets receive changed names.

The Django's staticfiles documentation notes that **ManifestStaticFilesStorage** is intended for production use, requires **DEBUG = False**, and depends on collectstatic having been run successfully. The benefit in this recipe is not only cleaner URLs. The benefit is that browsers and proxies can cache aggressively without serving stale files after a deploy, because the manifest-driven filenames change when the content changes.

Running Collectstatic

A production static-files solution is incomplete without the **collectstatic** step because that is the moment where the application's scattered static assets are assembled into the storage backend configured under staticfiles. Once **collectstatic** finishes, the reverse proxy or cloud storage layer can serve a single coherent tree of versioned assets instead of scanning app directories or project-level asset directories itself.

```
python manage.py collectstatic --noinput
```

Once the assets are collected, a reverse proxy such as Nginx can serve **/static/** directly from **STATIC_ROOT**, or a remote storage backend can expose the same collected files through a CDN or cloud bucket. The template layer remains clean in both cases because the **{% static %}** tag resolves URLs through the storage configured under **staticfiles** in **STORAGES**. The storage backend owns that detail. This is exactly why the **STORAGES** model is such a strong fit for production static files.

Serving Media outside Static Pipeline

The user-uploaded files deserve a different operational treatment because they are not deployed artifacts. They continue to arrive after the application is already live, and Django's deployment checklist explicitly warns that they are untrusted. A profile image, document attachment, or uploaded snippet file should be stored through the default storage backend and served from the media path only. The static files are collected assets. And, the media files are stored content. Once that line is drawn clearly, both security and maintenance become easier because the file lifecycle is no longer ambiguous.

The end result is simpler to reason about and much better aligned with the way Django currently expects production file handling to be expressed. The static assets now move through a clear build-and-collect path, user uploads remain separate, and the template layer stays stable regardless of whether the final production serving strategy is local or remote.

Recipe 6: Implementing HTTPS and SSL Certificates

A production deployment is not truly ready for users until it protects traffic in transit. The login credentials, session cookies, password reset links, and authenticated API calls all travel through the network path between the browser and the application, and that path should be encrypted and integrity-protected. HTTPS is therefore not only a trust signal. In our app, it matters even more because authentication, file uploads, and account management all depend on users being able to trust the connection they are using.

In this recipe, we are going to expand the HTTPS setup so it does more than obtain a certificate and redirect port 80. It also aligns the application settings with secure defaults, calls out the reverse-proxy boundary clearly, and points forward to Content Security Policy so transport security and browser-executed content policy can reinforce each other instead of living as separate concerns.

Obtaining Certificate and HTTPS Only Normal Entry

To start with, we first point the domain at the server, install Certbot and its Nginx integration, request the certificate, and let Nginx terminate TLS. The important thing here in this recipe, is that the application's public entry path becomes HTTPS-first from that point onward. The HTTP should redirect to HTTPS, and the reverse proxy should become the trusted component that owns TLS termination. Once we do that, Django can safely build on the assumption that secure requests are the norm rather than the exception.

```
sudo apt-get update
sudo apt-get install certbot python3-certbot-nginx
sudo certbot --nginx -d gitforgits.com -d www.gitforgits.com
```

Next, we want a working Nginx configuration which can send all plain HTTP traffic to the secure site and serve the HTTPS site with the obtained certificate. That is still the heart of the deployment pattern, because it moves the application into a security posture where encrypted transport is the baseline rather than a feature the user might or might not choose.

```
server {
    listen 80;
    server_name gitforgits.com www.gitforgits.com;
    return 301 https://$server_name$request_uri;
}
server {
    listen 443 ssl http2;
    server_name gitforgits.com www.gitforgits.com;
    ssl_certificate
/etc/letsencrypt/live/gitforgits.com/fullchain.pem;
    ssl_certificate_key
/etc/letsencrypt/live/gitforgits.com/privkey.pem;
    location / {
        proxy_pass http://127.0.0.1:8001;
        proxy_set_header Host $host;
        proxy_set_header X-Forwarded-Proto $scheme;
        proxy_set_header X-Real-IP $remote_addr;
```

```
        proxy_set_header X-Forwarded-For
$proxy_add_x_forwarded_for;
    }
}
```

Once the proxy owns that boundary, the application can start making stronger assumptions safely.

Matching Django's Secure Settings to HTTPS Deployment

Once Nginx terminates TLS and forwards requests to Django, the application settings need to reflect that deployment reality. For this, the secure cookies should be enabled, HTTP-to-HTTPS redirection should be active if the proxy is not already handling it exclusively, and the proxy header that signals HTTPS should be declared correctly. The HSTS can then be added so browsers remember that the site must only be loaded over HTTPS for a defined period.

```
SECURE_SSL_REDIRECT = True
SECURE_PROXY_SSL_HEADER = ("HTTP_X_FORWARDED_PROTO", "https")
SESSION_COOKIE_SECURE = True
CSRF_COOKIE_SECURE = True
SECURE_HSTS_SECONDS = 31536000
SECURE_HSTS_INCLUDE_SUBDOMAINS = True
SECURE_HSTS_PRELOAD = True
```

These above settings matter because the HTTPS is not only about the certificate file. It is about making the rest of the application behave as though transport security is guaranteed. Session cookies should not travel over insecure transport. The CSRF cookies too should not either. The Browsers should learn that the site is HTTPS-only. And, the requests forwarded from the proxy should be recognized as secure requests by Django. All of these pieces turn the deployment into a coherent security story rather than one certificate sitting on top of an otherwise ambiguous runtime.

Using HTTPS for Browser Security Policies

The final operational step is to validate both the Nginx configuration and the certificate renewal path. A secure setup that silently expires a certificate or contains a broken proxy configuration is not secure in practice. The testing of the configuration and a dry-run renewal remains an important part of the deployment routine. Once those pass, the application can trust that the secure transport boundary is stable enough for the stronger browser and session protections that follow.

```
sudo nginx -t
sudo systemctl reload nginx
sudo certbot renew --dry-run
```

It makes HTTPS the only normal entry path, it aligns Django's secure defaults with that deployment reality, and it points directly into CSP so the browser-side trust model grows from the same secure foundation rather than being bolted on later.

Recipe 7: Enforcing Content Security Policy

A strong CSP reduces the chance that injected or unexpected content will execute, which makes it an especially useful companion to the forms, authentication, and API features that GitforGits already depends on. In this recipe, we will enable the middleware, define a practical baseline policy, and show how nonce-aware templates work when inline scripts or styles are truly necessary.

Enabling Middleware and Defining Baseline Policy

For many Django applications, a practical baseline is to allow resources from the same origin, allow scripts from self plus request-specific nonces for the small number of inline scripts that remain, and keep styles similarly constrained. The Django 6.0 exposes this through **ContentSecurityPolicyMiddleware** and the **SECURE_CSP** setting. The middleware should sit in MIDDLEWARE, and the templates should receive the CSP context processor if we want to use nonces.

```
from django.utils.csp import CSP
MIDDLEWARE = [
    "django.middleware.security.SecurityMiddleware",
    "django.contrib.sessions.middleware.SessionMiddleware",
    "django.middleware.common.CommonMiddleware",
    "django.middleware.csrf.CsrfViewMiddleware",
    "django.contrib.auth.middleware.AuthenticationMiddleware",

"django.middleware.content.ContentSecurityPolicyMiddleware",
]
TEMPLATES = [
    {
```

```
        "BACKEND":
"django.template.backends.django.DjangoTemplates",
        "DIRS": [BASE_DIR / "templates"],
        "APP_DIRS": True,
        "OPTIONS": {
            "context_processors": [
                "django.template.context_processors.request",
                "django.template.context_processors.csp",
            ],
        },
    },
]
SECURE_CSP = {
    "default-src": [CSP.SELF],
    "script-src": [CSP.SELF, CSP.NONCE],
    "style-src": [CSP.SELF, CSP.NONCE],
    "img-src": [CSP.SELF, "data:"],
    "font-src": [CSP.SELF],
    "object-src": [CSP.NONE],
    "base-uri": [CSP.SELF],
    "frame-ancestors": [CSP.NONE],
}
```

This policy is strict enough to be meaningful without being impossible to adopt. The same-origin content is trusted, inline scripts and styles must carry a valid nonce to execute, object embedding is disabled, and framing is restricted. These are sensible defaults for a Django application that serves its own static assets and does not rely heavily on third-party script injection.

Using Nonces in Templates

A nonce only helps when inline content is genuinely necessary. When inline content is required, Django's **csp_nonce** variable can be inserted into the relevant **<script>** or **<style>** tag. The middleware then automatically adds the matching **nonce-<value>** source expression to the policy header for that response. The Django's CSP documentation also explains that nonce generation is lazy, meaning the nonce is created only if **{{ csp_nonce }}** is actually accessed during rendering. That is efficient, but it also means we need to think carefully about where nonce-bearing tags live. A cached template fragment that contains an old nonce can collide with the fresh header for a later response.

```
<script nonce="{{ csp_nonce }}">
    window.snippetId = "{{ snippet.id }}";
</script>
<style nonce="{{ csp_nonce }}">
    .snippet-card {
        border: 1px solid #ddd;
        padding: 1rem;
    }
</style>
```

A nonce-aware template is useful for transitional cases, small data handoffs, or narrowly scoped inline behavior, but it should not become a license to keep embedding large script blocks inside templates. The policy is strongest when the application serves most assets from static files and uses nonces only where there is a real reason to do so.

Rolling Out CSP and using Report-only Mode

A CSP is powerful enough that introducing it abruptly can break legitimate resources if the current application still depends on inline scripts, third-party assets, or sources the policy does not yet allow. The Django 6.0 accounts for this by supporting a report-only mode through **SECURE_CSP_REPORT_ONLY**, which sends the browser a monitoring policy instead of an enforced one. It gives valuable rollout path. We can observe where the current templates or static assets conflict with the intended policy, correct those areas, and then move to full enforcement once the application is ready.

```
SECURE_CSP_REPORT_ONLY = {
    "default-src": [CSP.SELF],
    "script-src": [CSP.SELF, CSP.NONCE],
    "style-src": [CSP.SELF, CSP.NONCE],
}
```

A report-only phase turns CSP adoption into a guided cleanup instead of a sudden outage. Once the reports are quiet and the templates have been adjusted, the enforcing policy can become the new baseline with much more confidence.

To sum up, the Django 6.0's built-in middleware, settings, and nonce support enforces the policy as part of its normal security configuration rather than relying on a separate package or custom response logic.

Summary

To conclude, we strengthened the final stages of taking a Django application from development into a production-ready state by focusing on testing, automation, deployment, and runtime security. We began by reinforcing the value of unit testing. From there, we automated the testing workflow so checks could run consistently under Python 3.12 during development and in shared CI environments. We then moved into production preparation, where we shaped environment-specific settings, externalized secrets and database configuration, and followed a more deliberate operational checklist.

Later, we updated the deployment flow with an ASGI-aware application path, a supervised process model, and a reverse proxy setup that fit modern Django deployment guidance more closely. After that, we secured traffic with HTTPS and SSL certificates, strengthened defaults for cookies and proxy-aware settings, and extended the security posture further through Content Security Policy with Django 6.0, including nonce-aware templates. In brief, we built a more complete understanding of how testing, deployment, storage, and security worked together in a production Django application.

CHAPTER 9: ADVANCED WEB APPLICATION FUNCTIONALITY

Overview

In this final chapter, we will explore features that make Django app feel richer, more interactive, and more capable in everyday use. We begin by extending the account experience through custom user profiles so our app can store and display information that goes beyond authentication and supports a more personalized interface. After that, we will work with Django's template system to generate dynamic content in a more structured way, using inheritance, reusable fragments, and cleaner state-preserving patterns. We will also build custom decorators for views so repeated access checks and shared behaviors can be reused consistently without cluttering individual view logic.

As the chapter progress, we will move into real-time application behavior by integrating Django channels and WebSockets through an ASGI-aware setup for live communication features. Finally, we will rebuild search using PostgreSQL's modern full-text search tools so the application can rank, highlight, and return more meaningful results across its data.

So, let us begin.

Recipe 1: Creating and Managing Custom User Profiles

While Django's authentication system gives us a dependable way to identify and authenticate users, most of the real applications eventually need more user-related data than the authentication model should reasonably hold by itself. Our app is a good example because, a user account may need a biography, a profile image, a public website, and additional presentation-oriented details that are important to the user experience but not central to authentication itself. A profile model is a strong fit for this kind of requirement because it lets us extend the account cleanly without overloading the custom user model with fields that belong more to personalization than to identity.

In this recipe, we will create a profile model that sits alongside the project's user model, make sure every account can be paired with a profile, and then shape the admin and template usage so profile information becomes easy to manage and easy to display across the application.

Defining Profile Model

The cleanest way to do, is to use **settings.AUTH_USER_MODEL** in **OneToOneField**. It keeps the relationship flexible and ensures the profile model stays correct even when the actual user model class is custom. The profile picture can continue to use **ImageField**, and the uploaded media will naturally flow through the default storage backend.

```
from django.conf import settings
```

```
from django.db import models
class UserProfile(models.Model):
    user = models.OneToOneField(
        settings.AUTH_USER_MODEL,
        on_delete=models.CASCADE,
        related_name="profile",
    )
    bio = models.TextField(max_length=500, blank=True)
    profile_picture = models.ImageField(
        upload_to="profile_pics/",
        null=True,
        blank=True,
    )
    website_url = models.URLField(blank=True, null=True)
    def __str__(self):
        return self.user.email
```

This model gives us a profile that is both practical and easy to reason about. The account owns the authentication and identity behavior, while the profile owns the personalization fields that help the rest of the application feel human and expressive. Here, a login screen does not need to know anything about profile pictures, while a profile page does not need to own the deeper details of password handling or permissions.

Creating Automatic Profile Records

Once the profile model exists, the next problem is making sure new users do not end up without a corresponding profile. The Django's model signals still provide a simple and familiar way to handle that automatically at account creation time. Instead of using the built-in user class as the signal sender, we should tie the signal to **`settings.AUTH_USER_MODEL`**. That keeps the receiver aligned with the actual user model registered in the project settings. The receiver only needs to create the profile when the user is first created. That keeps the behavior simple and avoids unnecessary save calls on every ordinary user update. The Django's signal system continues to support this model-level hook pattern cleanly, even though signals should still be used with discipline and only where the coupling is truly helpful.

```
from django.conf import settings
```

```
from django.db.models.signals import post_save
from django.dispatch import receiver
from .models import UserProfile
@receiver(post_save, sender=settings.AUTH_USER_MODEL)
def create_user_profile(sender, instance, created, **kwargs):
    if created:
        UserProfile.objects.create(user=instance)
```

This is enough to guarantee that new accounts receive profile rows automatically. We do not need a second signal that blindly saves the profile on every user save unless there is a very specific project requirement that justifies it. This design also makes it easier to backfill profiles for existing accounts if needed, because the creation rule is now very obvious and can be mirrored in a management command or one-time migration script later if the project ever needs it.

Profile Manageability in Admin

The admin integration can remain very simple because the profile object is already focused and descriptive. A short **ModelAdmin** with a few list columns is enough to make the data manageable by staff users. After that, the application's views and templates can treat the profile as a normal extension of the account by following the one-to-one relationship. The template layer benefits from the **related_name="profile"** we added earlier because it makes access readable.

We can display **request.user.profile.profile_picture.url** without building extra lookup machinery.

```
from django.contrib import admin
from .models import UserProfile
@admin.register(UserProfile)
class UserProfileAdmin(admin.ModelAdmin):
    list_display = ("user", "website_url")
    search_fields = ("user__email", "bio", "website_url")
{% if request.user.is_authenticated and request.user.profile
%}
    <section class="profile-summary">
        {% if request.user.profile.profile_picture %}
```

```
            <img src="{{
request.user.profile.profile_picture.url }}" alt="{{
request.user.email }}">
        {% endif %}
        <p>{{ request.user.profile.bio }}</p>
        {% if request.user.profile.website_url %}
            <a href="{{ request.user.profile.website_url
}}">{{ request.user.profile.website_url }}</a>
        {% endif %}
    </section>
{% endif %}
```

That kind of natural traversal is one of the quiet strengths of a well-designed relationship model. It keeps the view code lighter and the templates more expressive, especially when personalization starts appearing across several screens of the application.

The user profile is still a one-to-one extension of the account, it still supports personalization cleanly, and it still integrates naturally with admin, views, and templates. The important difference is that it now respects the project's custom user-model architecture and the modern file-handling approach already taught earlier.

Recipe 2: Generating Dynamic Content using Django Templates

Any app can get benefitted from dynamic content because the homepage, dashboard, snippet listings, and account views can all become more relevant when the interface reflects who the user is, what they are looking at, and how they arrived there. A signed-in user may see a welcome message, recent snippets, or profile-aware actions, while a visitor may see a lighter public view. A list page may need to preserve active filters while users paginate through results.

In this recipe, we will implement dynamic content using Django 6.0's stronger template toolkit. We will keep the inheritance in place, introducing partials for reusable fragments, and using the built-in **querystring** tag to preserve filter and pagination state cleanly. The **partialdef** and **partial** tags are built into Django 6.0, and the **querystring** tag can preserve, add, replace, or remove query parameters directly in templates.

Driving Personalized Content from View Context

The dynamic templates still begin with a simple rule, that the template can only render what the view gives it or what global context processors provide. A homepage greeting remains a useful example because it shows how a small amount of context can make the template feel personal without pushing business logic into the template itself. The template should not be deciding what time-of-day greeting applies. The view should do that work and pass the result as context.

```
from django.shortcuts import render
from django.utils import timezone
def home(request):
    current_hour = timezone.localtime().hour
    if current_hour < 12:
        greeting = "morning"
    elif current_hour < 18:
        greeting = "afternoon"
    else:
        greeting = "evening"
    context = {
        "greeting": greeting,
    }
    return render(request, "home.html", context)
{% if user.is_authenticated %}
    <p>Good {{ greeting }}, {{ user.email }}!</p>
{% else %}
    <p>Welcome to GitforGits.</p>
{% endif %}
```

This above keeps the dynamic content intentional and easy to test. The template displays the context, but it does not own the logic that generated it. Once multiple fragments on a page depend on context, the view remains the clean place to shape those values before the template handles the final presentation.

Using Inheritance for Repeated Fragments

Inheritance still belongs at the page-structure level. A base template should define the site shell, and child templates should fill in the blocks that differ from page to page. The built-in

partialdef and partial tags give us a direct way to define reusable template fragments and render them in the same template. In our app, a **snippet-preview** card is an excellent example because it can appear in search results, on a dashboard, and on user profile pages without forcing us to keep copying the same markup.

```
<!-- base.html -->
<!DOCTYPE html>
<html>
<head>
    <title>{% block title %}GitforGits{% endblock %}</title>
</head>
<body>
    <header>
        <h1>GitforGits</h1>
    </header>
    <main>
        {% block content %}{% endblock %}
    </main>
</body>
</html>
{% extends "base.html" %}
{% block title %}Your Snippets{% endblock %}
{% block content %}
    {% partialdef snippet_card %}
        <article class="snippet-card">
            <h3>{{ snippet.title }}</h3>
            <p>{{ snippet.code|truncatechars:120 }}</p>
            <a href="{% url 'snippets:snippet_detail'
snippet.id %}">Read more</a>
        </article>
    {% endpartialdef %}
```

```
    <section class="snippet-list">
        {% for snippet in snippets %}
            {% partial snippet_card %}
        {% empty %}
            <p>No snippets found.</p>
        {% endfor %}
    </section>
{% endblock %}
```

This pattern gives the template two useful layers of reuse. The inheritance defines the stable page shell, and **`partials`** define the repeated content fragment. It is a much cleaner fit for modern Django templates than forcing every repeated HTML block into either a separate included file or a copied block of markup. It also keeps the template readable because the repeated fragment has a name and a purpose instead of being rediscovered in every loop.

Preserving Filters and Pagination with 'Querystring' Tag

This dynamic content often becomes frustrating too if the page loses the state the user just chose. A filtered snippet list is the most common example. A user may filter by language, move to page two, and then discover that the pagination links dropped the filter, or that a new filter cleared every existing query parameter. The Django 6.0's built-in **`querystring`** tag fixes that elegantly. It lets the template preserve the current query string while replacing or removing just the parameter we care about.

```
<nav class="filters">
    <a href="{% querystring language='python' page=1
%}">Python</a>
    <a href="{% querystring language='javascript' page=1
%}">JavaScript</a>
    <a href="{% querystring language=None page=1 %}">All</a>
</nav>
{% if page_obj.has_previous %}
    <a href="{% querystring page=page_obj.previous_page_number
%}">Previous</a>
{% endif %}
```

```
<span>Page {{ page_obj.number }} of {{
page_obj.paginator.num_pages }}</span>
{% if page_obj.has_next %}
    <a href="{% querystring page=page_obj.next_page_number
%}">Next</a>
{% endif %}
```

This now makes the template much cleaner than older approaches that stitched strings together by hand. It also reduces subtle bugs because the tag understands how to preserve existing parameters, replace values, and remove keys by assigning None. Once we adopt this pattern, dynamic list pages become easier to maintain and easier for users to trust. They can move through the data without rebuilding their browsing state every time they click.

To conclude, the page can still be personalized through context and inheritance, but **`partials`** and the **`querystring`** tag now make the **`dynamic-template`** story significantly stronger and more maintainable.

Recipe 3: Building Custom Decorators for Views

It's getting harder and harder to apply the same checks or procedures to different views. Take this example wherein, we might want to restrict editing and deleting of snippets to only the people who wrote them. We might also want to keep track of who's seen which views for auditing purposes. In this recipe, with the help of Python decorators, we will make our views more consistent and cleaner, and encapsulate and reuse common functionality. If we avoid using standard code, we can use custom decorators to wrap up functionality around our view logic.

Creating Custom Decorator

A decorator is a function that takes another function as an argument and extends its behavior without explicitly modifying it. Suppose we want to create a decorator that ensures only the author of a snippet can edit or delete it. We can create a decorator that checks this condition and either proceeds with the view or redirects the user with an error message.

```
from django.http import HttpResponseForbidden
from django.shortcuts import get_object_or_404, redirect
from .models import Snippet
def user_is_snippet_author(view_func):
```

```
def _wrapped_view_func(request, *args, **kwargs):
snippet = get_object_or_404(Snippet, pk=kwargs['pk'])
if snippet.author != request.user:
return HttpResponseForbidden()
return view_func(request, *args, **kwargs)
return _wrapped_view_func
```

This decorator first retrieves the snippet based on the **pk** argument expected in the view's keyword arguments. It then checks if the current user is the author of the snippet. If not, it returns a **HttpResponseForbidden**, otherwise, it proceeds with the original view function.

Applying Decorator to Views

To apply our custom decorator, we will simply wrap our view functions with it. For class-based views, we need to use the **method_decorator** helper.

```
from django.utils.decorators import method_decorator
from django.views.generic import UpdateView
from .models import Snippet
from .decorators import user_is_snippet_author
@method_decorator(user_is_snippet_author, name='dispatch')
class SnippetUpdateView(UpdateView):
 model = Snippet
 fields = ['title', 'code']
 template_name = 'snippets/edit.html'
```

For function-based views, we can apply the decorator directly above the view definition.

```
@user_is_snippet_author
def edit_snippet(request, pk):
 # View logic here
```

We have to ensure thorough testing of our decorator by creating unit tests that verify both the permitted and forbidden paths work as expected. This could involve mocking user requests to the decorated view and asserting the correct responses are returned based on the user's relationship to the snippet.

Recipe 4: Implementing Real-time Features using Django Channels

Features like notifications, live collaboration signals, room presence, and activity updates are all examples of features that benefit from long-lived connections and asynchronous message handling. And, that is where Django channels fits naturally. The channels extends Django's ASGI support so the project can handle protocols such as **`WebSockets`** alongside ordinary HTTP, which makes it a strong fit for real-time features.

In this recipe, we will wire channels into the project cleanly, use an ASGI-first application structure, and configure a channel layer that works well in development and also has a production-ready path.

Installing Channels with ASGI Server

The cleanest setup path is to install channels together with Daphne so the project gets an ASGI-capable runserver command during development. After that, we add channels itself and the app that will contain our consumers.

```
python -m pip install -U "channels[daphne]" channels-redis
INSTALLED_APPS = [
    "daphne",
    "django.contrib.admin",
    "django.contrib.auth",
    "django.contrib.contenttypes",
    "django.contrib.sessions",
    "django.contrib.messages",
    "django.contrib.staticfiles",
    "channels",
    "chat",
]
```

In the above, we install the ASGI server intentionally, we register it intentionally, and the project knows exactly which part is providing the development WebSocket-capable server. Once the apps are installed, the rest of the work becomes about wiring protocols and message routing rather than fighting missing runtime components.

Switching to ASGI-First Routing Structure

The channels builds on Django's ASGI support, which means the project should expose a single ASGI application that knows how to handle both ordinary HTTP traffic and **WebSocket** traffic. The current channels installation guidance shows a **ProtocolTypeRouter** wrapping **get_asgi_application()** for HTTP, and then layering **WebSocket** routing onto the same root application. This is an important update because it keeps HTTP and WebSocket behavior under one coherent ASGI entry point rather than treating WebSockets as a disconnected side system.

```
# gitforgits/asgi.py
import os
from channels.auth import AuthMiddlewareStack
from channels.routing import ProtocolTypeRouter, URLRouter
from channels.security.websocket import
AllowedHostsOriginValidator
from django.core.asgi import get_asgi_application
from chat.routing import websocket_urlpatterns
os.environ.setdefault("DJANGO_SETTINGS_MODULE",
"gitforgits.settings")
django_asgi_app = get_asgi_application()
application = ProtocolTypeRouter(
    {
        "http": django_asgi_app,
        "websocket": AllowedHostsOriginValidator(
            AuthMiddlewareStack(
                URLRouter(websocket_urlpatterns)
            )
        ),
    }
)
ASGI_APPLICATION = "gitforgits.asgi.application"
```

Once this file is in place, the project has a clear root application for both development and deployment. The above structure is stronger than a minimal **ProtocolTypeRouter** because it adds two layers that matter in a real application. The **AuthMiddlewareStack** powers **WebSocket** consumers access the authenticated user through the connection scope, and **AllowedHostsOriginValidator** helps enforce origin checks based on the project's allowed hosts. These both two layers are exactly the kind of practical hardening that is useful beyond a toy echo server.

Configuring Channel Layer

A real-time feature often needs more than a single consumer handling one connection. Once we want to broadcast notifications, send a message to a room, or communicate across multiple worker processes, we need a channel layer. The channels supports an in-memory layer for development and testing, but its own documentation is explicit that this should not be used in production. For production, **channels_redis** is the official Django-maintained channel layer backend. It gives a clean two-stage path, wherein we keep development simple with the in-memory backend when we are only experimenting locally, and then we move to Redis when the project is deployed or when multiple processes must coordinate.

For example, in development:

```
CHANNEL_LAYERS = {
    "default": {
        "BACKEND": "channels.layers.InMemoryChannelLayer",
    }
}
```

And then, in production:

```
CHANNEL_LAYERS = {
    "default": {
        "BACKEND": "channels_redis.core.RedisChannelLayer",
        "CONFIG": {
            "hosts": [("127.0.0.1", 6379)],
        },
    }
}
```

This separation keeps the learning path smooth.

Creating Simple Notification Consumer and Route

With the runtime in place, we can now build the first feature. A notification-style consumer is a good fit because it shows how a user-specific group can be joined at connection time and then used for later pushes.

```
# chat/consumers.py
import json
from channels.generic.websocket import AsyncWebsocketConsumer
class NotificationConsumer(AsyncWebsocketConsumer):
    async def connect(self):
        if self.scope["user"].is_anonymous:
            await self.close()
            return
        self.group_name = f"user_{self.scope['user'].pk}"
        await self.channel_layer.group_add(self.group_name,
self.channel_name)
        await self.accept()
    async def disconnect(self, close_code):
        if hasattr(self, "group_name"):
            await
self.channel_layer.group_discard(self.group_name,
self.channel_name)
    async def notify(self, event):
        await self.send(
            text_data=json.dumps(
                {
                    "type": "notification",
                    "message": event["message"],
                }
            )
        )
```

```
# chat/routing.py
from django.urls import path
from .consumers import NotificationConsumer
websocket_urlpatterns = [
    path("ws/notifications/", NotificationConsumer.as_asgi()),
]
```

This above thing ultimately completes the modern channels setup. With this, our app now has a proper ASGI application, a clear channel layer story, and a consumer that is structured around real application behavior.

Recipe 5: Implementing WebSockets

Once channels is wired into the project, the next step is to shape an actual WebSocket feature that feels like part of our app. A chat room is still a good teaching example because it exercises the full-duplex nature of WebSockets clearly, like the users are connecting, messages are received, messages are broadcast to the room group, and clients update immediately without page refreshes.

In this recipe, we will now match WebSocket with the current channels setup for modern deployment rather than an isolated or outdated runtime pattern.

Defining Room-based Websocket Route and Consumer

Well, for a chat room, the route should carry the room identifier, and the consumer should derive the group name from that identifier so all participants in the same room join the same broadcast channel. It keeps the behavior easy to understand. The URL names the room, the consumer joins the room group, and every message sent to the group is broadcast back to connected clients. The channels' consumer abstraction remains the clearest way to express that behavior, and the group-based channel layer pattern is exactly what the current tutorial and channel-layer guidance continue to build around.

```
# chat/routing.py
from django.urls import path
from .consumers import ChatConsumer
websocket_urlpatterns = [
    path("ws/chat/<str:room_name>/", ChatConsumer.as_asgi()),
]
```

```
# chat/consumers.py
import json
from channels.generic.websocket import AsyncWebsocketConsumer
class ChatConsumer(AsyncWebsocketConsumer):
    async def connect(self):
        self.room_name =
self.scope["url_route"]["kwargs"]["room_name"]
        self.room_group_name = f"chat_{self.room_name}"
        await self.channel_layer.group_add(
            self.room_group_name,
            self.channel_name,
        )
        await self.accept()
    async def disconnect(self, close_code):
        await self.channel_layer.group_discard(
            self.room_group_name,
            self.channel_name,
        )
    async def receive(self, text_data):
        payload = json.loads(text_data)
        message = payload["message"]
        sender = self.scope["user"].email if
self.scope["user"].is_authenticated else "guest"
        await self.channel_layer.group_send(
            self.room_group_name,
            {
                "type": "chat_message",
                "message": message,
                "sender": sender,
            },
```

```
        )
    async def chat_message(self, event):
        await self.send(
            text_data=json.dumps(
                {
                    "message": event["message"],
                    "sender": event["sender"],
                }
            )
        )
```

This consumer reflects the modern channels structure cleanly. It derives room state from the route, uses the channel layer for broadcast, and can also see the authenticated user because the project ASGI application already wrapped WebSocket traffic with AuthMiddlewareStack previously. That is exactly why the earlier ASGI wiring matters so much.

Connecting Browser to Websocket Client

A modern WebSocket example should also respect the deployment environment. If the page is served over HTTPS, the browser should connect with **wss://**, not **ws://**. If the page is served locally without HTTPS during development, then **ws://** is fine. The client-side code should therefore derive the scheme from the current page instead of hard-coding one transport.

```
<script>
const roomName = JSON.parse(document.getElementById("room-name").textContent);
const wsScheme = window.location.protocol === "https:" ? "wss" : "ws";
const chatSocket = new WebSocket(

`${wsScheme}://${window.location.host}/ws/chat/${roomName}/`
);
chatSocket.onmessage = function (e) {
    const data = JSON.parse(e.data);
    const log = document.querySelector("#chat-log");
```

```
    log.value += `${data.sender}: ${data.message}\n`;
};
chatSocket.onclose = function () {
    console.error("Chat socket closed unexpectedly");
};
document.querySelector("#chat-message-submit").onclick =
function () {
    const input = document.querySelector("#chat-message-
input");
    const message = input.value.trim();
    if (!message) {
        return;
    }
    chatSocket.send(JSON.stringify({ message }));
    input.value = "";
};
</script>
```

This frontend stays intentionally narrow. It chooses the correct WebSocket scheme, opens the connection, appends received messages, and sends new ones.

Deploying App through ASGI Server

The application needs an ASGI-capable server that understands both HTTP and WebSocket traffic. The channels' current deployment documentation highlights Daphne as the official project-maintained HTTP/WebSocket server and explains that it can serve both protocols directly. It also notes that other ASGI servers can work as long as they follow the ASGI spec.

Hence, the simplest production framing for a channels-enabled project is therefore to run Daphne behind Nginx and let Daphne serve both HTTP and WebSocket traffic from the same ASGI application. The cookies and session behavior remains aligned because both protocols stay on the same application boundary.

```
daphne -b 127.0.0.1 -p 8001 gitforgits.asgi:application
```

After this, a matching Nginx reverse-proxy block should pass upgrade headers so WebSocket connections can be established correctly:

```
location /ws/ {
    proxy_pass http://127.0.0.1:8001;
    proxy_http_version 1.1;
    proxy_set_header Upgrade $http_upgrade;
    proxy_set_header Connection "upgrade";
    proxy_set_header Host $host;
    proxy_set_header X-Forwarded-Proto $scheme;
}
```

With this, the application now has one ASGI entry point, one WebSocket routing scheme, and one deployment shape that can actually carry the feature into production without changing the entire architecture later.

Recipe 6: Performing Efficient Full-text Search

A Full-text Search is one of the places where a content-heavy application either feels powerful or feels frustrating. Our app needs search that can do more than match one field with a simple icontains filter. The users should be able to search across titles, descriptions, and code-related text in a way that ranks relevant results higher, highlights useful snippets of text, and scales better than naive pattern matching once the dataset expands.

In ths recipe, we will use Django 6.0's PostgreSQL search API to support a modern search engine without requiring an external search engine from the start. We will start with weighted annotated vectors, rank the results, highlight them, and add a functional GIN index that matches the vector expression.

Modeling Fields and Adding GIN Index

A good full-text search design begins by deciding which fields should actually contribute to relevance. The Django's current PostgreSQL search guidance explicitly supports a functional GIN index that matches the search vector expression itself, and that is usually the stronger first pattern when all the searchable fields live on one model. The PostgreSQL then indexes the same weighted search expression we will use in the **`queryset`**.

```
from django.contrib.postgres.indexes import GinIndex
from django.contrib.postgres.search import SearchVector
from django.db import models
```

```
class Snippet(models.Model):
    title = models.CharField(max_length=100)
    description = models.TextField(blank=True)
    code = models.TextField()
    class Meta:
        indexes = [
            GinIndex(
                SearchVector("title", weight="A",
config="english")
                + SearchVector("description", weight="B",
config="english")
                + SearchVector("code", weight="C",
config="english"),
                name="snippet_search_gin",
            ),
        ]
```

In the above, the app can perform weighted full-text queries efficiently, and the index is directly aligned with the actual search expression. The model now expresses not only which fields are searchable, but also which fields matter more for ranking. It makes the search behavior more intentional and far more useful than a flat match across every text column.

Building Weighted Search Queryset

A modern full-text search view should not stop at "***did the row match or not?***" It should also rank matches and generate a useful snippet of highlighted text so users can see why the result appeared. Both, the PostgreSQL and Django handle this very well through **`SearchVector`**, **`SearchQuery`**, **`SearchRank`**, and **`SearchHeadline`**. In our app, the practical default for user-entered search strings is **`search_type="websearch"`** as it handles terms and common search-style operators in a way that feels more natural for ordinary text input. After this, we can then annotate the **`queryset`** with rank and a highlighted headline, filter out weak matches, and order the results from strongest to weakest.

```
from django.contrib.postgres.search import (
    SearchHeadline,
    SearchQuery,
```

```
    SearchRank,
    SearchVector,
)
from django.shortcuts import render
from .models import Snippet
def search_snippets(request):
    query_string = request.GET.get("q", "").strip()
    results = Snippet.objects.none()
    if query_string:
        vector = (
            SearchVector("title", weight="A",
config="english")
            + SearchVector("description", weight="B",
config="english")
            + SearchVector("code", weight="C",
config="english")
        )
        query = SearchQuery(query_string,
search_type="websearch", config="english")
        results = (
            Snippet.objects.annotate(
                rank=SearchRank(vector, query,
cover_density=True),
                headline=SearchHeadline(
                    "description",
                    query,
                    start_sel="<mark>",
                    stop_sel="</mark>",
                    max_fragments=2,
                ),
            )
```

```
            .filter(rank__gte=0.05)
            .order_by("-rank", "-id")
        )
    return render(
        request,
        "snippets/search_results.html",
        {
            "query": query_string,
            "results": results,
        },
    )
```

This above queryset is quite a strong for three reasons:

- It weights fields by importance,
- It ranks the results instead of returning a flat unstructured list, and
- It provides highlighted description fragments the template can render directly.

All these creates a much more useful search interface for users. The **cover_density=True** option also improves ranking by giving more credit to results where the matching terms appear closer together. That kind of ranking refinement is exactly what helps full-text search feel meaningfully better than basic substring matching.

Structuring Search Logic using 'Lexeme'

A plain **SearchQuery** is often enough, but Django 6.0 now also supports Lexeme, which is especially useful when the application wants to combine search terms structurally without trusting raw operator syntax from the user. With its help, instead of asking users to provide raw PostgreSQL search syntax, we can construct a structured query from terms we control in Python.

```
from django.contrib.postgres.search import Lexeme,
SearchQuery, SearchVector

def advanced_search_snippets(request):
    include_term = request.GET.get("include", "").strip()
    optional_term = request.GET.get("optional", "").strip()
    exclude_term = request.GET.get("exclude", "").strip()
    vector = (
```

```
        SearchVector("title", weight="A", config="english")
        + SearchVector("description", weight="B",
config="english")
        + SearchVector("code", weight="C", config="english")
    )
    query_expression = None
    if include_term:
        query_expression = Lexeme(include_term)
    if optional_term:
        optional_expression = Lexeme(optional_term)
        query_expression = optional_expression if
query_expression is None else (query_expression |
optional_expression)
    if exclude_term:
        exclude_expression = ~Lexeme(exclude_term)
        query_expression = exclude_expression if
query_expression is None else (query_expression &
exclude_expression)
    results = Snippet.objects.none()
    if query_expression is not None:
        results = Snippet.objects.annotate(
            rank=SearchRank(vector,
SearchQuery(query_expression), cover_density=True)
        ).filter(rank__gt=0).order_by("-rank")
    return render(request,
"snippets/advanced_search_results.html", {"results": results})
```

The above is an excellent example of a modern pattern which did not exist in older Django versions. The search logic is still expressive, but the application constructs it safely rather than asking the user to hand-author a raw search expression.

Triggering 'Searchvectorfield'

A fully materialized **SearchVectorField** is still available, and it as a valid option when annotated search becomes too slow. However, the field must then be maintained, often through triggers. That means the best optimum path is to start with weighted vectors and a functional GIN index, then move to **SearchVectorField** only if profiling shows a real need for that extra complexity. It also means, that the project gets a powerful, ranked, highlighted search system immediately, and it reserves the trigger-maintained vector path for the moment when the dataset or workload actually justifies it.

Summary

Summing up, we learned how Django supported richer application behavior beyond standard pages and forms. We began by extending the account system with custom user profiles, which allowed GitforGits to store and present more personalized information without overloading the authentication model itself. From there, we worked with Django's template system to generate more dynamic content by shaping views, templates, inheritance, and reusable fragments. We also used custom decorators to apply repeated view behavior, such as access rules and common processing logic.

The chapter then moved into real-time communication and richer discovery features. We learned how Django channels extended the project into an ASGI-aware, event-driven application for live notifications and room-based communication through WebSockets. We also saw modern WebSocket deployment patterns. And lastly, we rebuilt full-text search with modern PostgreSQL search tools, using weighted vectors, ranking, headlines, and safer structured query patterns so users could find the most relevant snippets more effectively.

Index

P

R

S

T

U

V

W

Epilogue

Finishing a technical book is not quite the same as finishing anything else.

A novel ends and you set it down. A course ends and you close the tab. But a book like this one ends somewhere different, somewhere less tidy and more honest. You close it not with the feeling of having consumed something, but with the feeling of having been changed by it, incrementally, recipe by recipe, problem by problem, until the way you think about building software has quietly shifted without your having noticed the moment it happened.

That shift is worth pausing to name, because it is easy to underestimate.

When most developers first encounter Django, they see a framework the way a newcomer sees any large system: as a collection of parts. There is a router. There are models. There is a template engine, a form library, an admin interface, a middleware stack. The parts are visible before the discipline that holds them together becomes clear. What changes is the recognition that Django is not primarily a collection of features but a set of positions about how web software should be built. It has opinions about where validation belongs. It has opinions about how authentication should be woven into the request cycle rather than bolted on top of it. It has opinions about the relationship between a model and the database behind it, between a view and the template it drives, between a form and the user it is trying to protect. Those opinions are not arbitrary. They were formed across years of real application development, and they encode hard-won lessons about what makes software maintainable, auditable, and safe to grow.

That is why the work that matters most does not happen inside this book. It happens after it.

The recipes you have worked through gave you a vocabulary. They gave you tested patterns for data modeling, views, templates, forms, authentication, APIs, background tasks, real-time features, search, security, and deployment. Taken one at a time, each of those patterns solved a specific problem. Taken together, they offered something more durable: a way of approaching Django that favors explicitness over magic, structure over improvisation, and long-term readability over short-term convenience. That way of approaching the framework does not expire when you close the book. It travels with you.

Django itself deserves some credit here. It is a framework that tends to reward developers who work with it honestly. When you resist the temptation to work around its patterns in favor of something that seems faster in the moment, it gives back readability, testability, and predictability over time. When you trust its conventions around authentication, permissions, and form handling, you get security that is woven into the structure of the application rather than depending on developer vigilance at every individual entry point. When you use its migration system, its ORM, and its template layer as they were designed to be used rather than as obstacles to route around, the application stays coherent across growth and change. That coherence is not glamorous. It does not appear in changelogs. But it is the quality that separates codebases that remain maintainable from codebases that gradually become systems no one fully understands anymore.

The final habit this book can encourage is also the simplest one. ***Keep building***.

Not to produce features, though features matter. Not to meet deadlines, though deadlines are real. It is build to deepen your relationship with the framework. It is build until the decisions that currently require deliberate thought become instinct. It is build until you can feel, early in a project, when a data model is drifting away from the domain it is supposed to represent, or when a view is absorbing responsibility that belongs in a form or a model method, or when a template is being asked to reason about things that should have been resolved before the render cycle began. That kind of perception is not something any book can hand you directly. It accumulates through repetition, through mistakes examined rather than simply moved past, through the specific kind of attention that comes from caring about the quality of what you build even when no one would notice the difference.

The recipes in this book were never the destination. They were the practice material for a way of thinking that you will now take into work this book could not anticipate or describe. The next codebase will present its own terrain. The patterns will travel. The judgment will sharpen. The work will continue.

That is exactly where a good technical book should leave you. Not at the end of something, but standing at the edge of what comes next, better equipped than you were when you began, and ready to build.

My best wishes to you and keep Django'ing your ideas!!

Thank You

www.ingramcontent.com/pod-product-compliance
Lightning Source LLC
Chambersburg PA
CBHW080212170726
48282CB00030B/1086
* 9 7 8 9 3 4 9 1 7 4 0 8 5 *